W9-BED-836

BACH AND THE BAROQUE

A Performing Guide to
Baroque Music with Special
Emphasis on the Music of
J. S. Bach

"A vibrant performance of any type of music is contingent upon the recognition and projection of its inner qualities. Foremost among these are the rhythms intended by the composer. and these are precisely the qualities that are the hardest to discover through the inadequate symbols of musical notation. Only by finding the missing links between the written notes and the living rhythms they once symbolized can we arrive at a means of making the revival of Baroque music a resuscitation rather than a mere reconstruction."

Putnam Aldrich, *Rhythm in the 17th-century Italian Monody*

BACH AND THE BAROQUE

A Performing Guide to Baroque Music with Special Emphasis on the Music of J. S. Bach

by Anthony Newman

PENDRAGON PRESS

Stuyvesant, NY

Series from Pendragon Press:

The Sociology of Music
Aesthetics in Music
French Opera in The 17th & 18th Centuries
The Juilliard Performance Guides
Thematic Catalogues
Film Retrospectives
Annotated Reference Tools in Music
Festschrift Series
Monographs in Musicology

The Historical Harpsichord.

Library of Congress Cataloging in Publication Data

Newman, Anthony.
  Bach and the baroque.

  Bibliography: p.
  Includes index.
  1. Bach, Johann Sebastian, 1685–1750. Works.
2. Music—Performance. 3. Music—17th century—History
and criticism. 4. Music—18th century—History and
criticism. I. Title.
MT92.B1N48   1985   780'.92'4   84-27392
ISBN 0-918728-46-0

2nd Printing 1986

Table of Contents

This book is dedicated to my family:
Mary Jane, Geoffrey, Matthew and Anthony,
and to all my students

Introduction

This text may be used as main material for a course on the performance of the music of J.S. Bach, or for a course on Baroque performance practice in general.

In tracing the development of Baroque performance practice research in this century we must mention the names Arnold Dolmetsch, Thurston Dart and Robert Donington. Since the 1950's there have been many names in both American and European scholarship that have contributed to performance practice research in Baroque music. They have brought to light source material of the Baroque via translation, commentary, or both. To them, I am grateful.

Most articles written about performance practice deal with relatively small areas (trills, overdotting, etc.) placing emphasis on citing original sources, or collating several original sources in order to implement a given position. There is not sufficient information in these articles to deal with all aspects of Baroque style. This text was built on the premise that as many conclusions as possible should be drawn from the sources themselves. Leaps to conclusions about other aspects of style insufficiently documented in sources are made on the basis of the author's own experience as performer.

There are different conclusions that one can reach, as the area is large, and some aspects of style find the various sources in disagreement (e.g., time signatures) or are simply not discussed. Most of the source disagreements stem from national differences in style.

I have incorporated footnotes into the text, citing the source and often the page.

I am especially indebted to Dorothy Barnhouse, a fine singer, linguist and German scholar. She acted as collaborator, translator, and editor. As a matter of fact, she occupied an all but co-author's position. Her suggestions, help, and encouragement made this book possible. I am also grateful to Richard Troeger, Scott Johnson, Gary Schultz, Edward Thompson, Maura Robinson, Alice Eaton Harris, Sara Doniach, Laurette Goldberg, Susan Shapiro, Clifford Gilmore, and Raphael Druian for their suggestions and comments, with a very special thanks to my wife, Mary Jane, to Howard Schott for his perspicacious reading of the manuscript, and to Kathryn Mackes for typing the manuscript. Finally, thanks to Richard Troeger and Marion Shepp for their contributions: the chapters on "Dance" and "Symbolism in General," respectively.

Problems of Biases
and Drawing Conclusions

Biases can cause immense problems. If we are accustomed to hearing things in a certain way, we become biased about the way they should sound. Music is one of the areas that is most subject to biases because the enjoyment of music for any individual has to do with a balance between the familiar and the unfamiliar, the predictable and the unpredictable. If, for instance, we are used to hearing Wagner's *Wedding March* played at "church" tempo and then hear it in the context of the opera *Lohengrin* (Act III), it sounds too fast. Hearing something familiar played in an unfamiliar way can cause great problems due to the fact that the energy needed simply to hear the piece in a new manner is spent instead on comparing the old and new manners of performance.

A good example of this problem is the opening bar of the *Toccata and Fugue in D Minor*, S. 565, which has usually been played or heard:

Example 1: Bach: Toccata and Fugue in D Minor, S. 565

However, any study of 18th century beat patterns will show that placing an accent on the C sharp is impossible. Unless specifically marked by a slur, the natural order of accentuation would prevail, that is, alternating strong and weak beats at every level:

Example 2

The first of every four notes is always accented more than the third. Consequently it certainly should be played:

2

Example 3: Bach: Toccata and Fugue in D Minor, S. 565

Adagio

Yet for those of us—and I have to include myself—who have been used to hearing this passage with stylistically incorrect accentuation and slurring, a great deal of exposure is necessary before we are able to hear and accept it in the "new" way.

When familiar elements of music are altered, similar problems are created. One example of this is the area of unequal notes, or inequality. (This subject is taken up in more detail later. (see p. 89) This particular area is enormously subject to the problem of biases. If, for instance, we have been used to hearing a piece played in rhythmically even fashion and then suddenly hear it played with altered rhythms, we have a big mental adjustment to make before we can hear the unaccustomed rhythmic pattern, much less react to it directly or make any judgments about it.

Another problem in music is the traditional mystique surrounding a composer or attitude of reverence with which we regard him. If we look at Bach through the early 20th century eyes of Schweitzer, we see him as a mystical, pious Lutheran. But, in a so-called "modern man's view," that of Friedrich Blume, editor of MGG *(Musik in Geschichte und Gegenwart),* Bach was in fact not like that at all. According to Blume, we do not know whether Bach was religious or irreligious.

Many other conceptions which we have taken for granted regarding composers may not be true at all. People of differing types attach quite different sentiments to Bach and his music. If we are religious, we might see in his music a kind of religious quality. In fact, we tend to project onto him and his music many different kinds of personal feelings we happen to have. As a result, it is hard for us to believe that these qualities do not originate in Bach and in his music. It is often very difficult for us to free ourselves from strictures of this sort, and one may well ask whether it is even desirable or necessary to do so. But we should at least try to become aware of what indeed comes from Bach, and what comes from the personal myths which we attach to him or his music.

Another problem that we encounter with Bach's music might be termed "miniaturization." By this I mean a reduction of any factor that would affect the correct or ideal energy level of a musical composition. In general, one can say that "miniaturization" occurs when the proper or needed insight into the performance of any music is lacking. This insight can be historical, structural or technical. Even an improper instrument tends to miniaturize. An incorrect edition tends to reduce or miniaturize the energy of the composition. Here are some more specific ways that miniaturization manifests itself.

A. *The building of "unfaithful" copies of Baroque instruments,* and especially of organs, has been affected by this miniaturization. (see p. 188) I believe it results either from a lack of knowledge or from a reverential attitude of unwillingness to question long-accepted beliefs. The music itself becomes altered when played on inappropriate instruments.

B. *Miniaturization in performance* occurs if we do not add proper stylistic ornamentation or if we neglect to fill out voices when needed. Sometimes we omit these because we are afraid to tamper with the printed page or are ignorant of the ornamental style. This is not just a recent problem, it seems to have concerned musicians during Bach's lifetime as well. Mattheson said in 1731 (writing about Kirchmaier and Falke, who had written about music 40 or 50 years earlier),

> ... even back in those days clever people noticed that it was not enough to play the *General-Bass* "correctly," that is, without mistakes, but that it had to be brought out artfully and decoratively ... Even though this was known 50 years ago, rather than taking the trouble to read (not to mention study) what these fine people have written on the subject, these useless fellows [clavier players] would prefer to bite off one of their own fingers, of which they could well afford to do without a few, since they do not know how to use all of them as they should ... those with empty shelves in their brains who criticize those who play with more than three fingers on the keyboard at once.
> (Mattheson, *Grosse General-Bass Schule,* pp. 8-9)

Miniaturization can also occur whenever one plays under tempo, under registration (on the organ), or with too little or no rubato. The reverse can also happen. All of these factors can be exaggerated or overdone; however, miniaturization is by far the more common error. If we want to be "safe," we restrict tempi (never play "too fast" or "too slow"), registration or rubato. We hear the music in a reduced or limited fashion. This makes it less possible for the original emotional energy to come out of the music. The idea of an "urtext" performance, i.e., a performance in which the text is in no way altered, is very much a part of the present day

4   PROBLEMS OF BIASES AND DRAWING CONCLUSIONS

aesthetic. Performers are often criticized for playing too slow or too fast, but, as we will see, the source material tells us surprising things, especially about tempi, which, in many instances, seem to have been either faster or slower than traditionally associated with the Baroque. It is probably a modern feeling that the really slow tempo in music—the very slow adagio —does not arrive until Beethoven's time. There are places in Bach's music where that kind of extremely slow tempo seems appropriate, especially when an indication such as "adagissimo" occurs.

Example 4: O Mensch bewein dein Sünde gross, S. 622

adagissimo

Another interesting bias is a strong dislike of metrical accents (a bias which influenced me until I understood what they do and how they actually function in the music). I am referring to certain kinds of rubatos which are based on the concept of "strong/weak" as this pertains to measures or to beats. When we discover how strong/weak measures and strong/weak beats work (see p. 58), we see how they force metrical accents to occur; these accents, incidentally, are often indicated in the music either by a filling out of the texture, or by ornamentation which will naturally take a certain time away from tempo.

Sources
. . . and what kinds of conclusions
may be drawn from them

When we attempt to draw conclusions from the source material as it might pertain to Bach's music several problems arise. Because Bach wrote nothing about the performance of his own works, we have to go to his contemporaries, friends, relatives and students. We will never be able to know exactly how Bach played his own music. Even if there were a student of his alive today whom we could question directly and who could demonstrate for us, our knowledge would still be inexact, since the information would be filtered through his own gift, his biases and his memory. It is quite impossible to know exactly how a composer wants something to sound unless he is present in the flesh to tell us. But even if Bach himself were alive to demonstrate, any given piece would not be performed the same way twice in a row; I believe this is especially true given the 18th century aesthetic and its high proclivity towards improvisation. We know from contemporary composers that some of them are very dictatorial and would like to control every detail of performance, while others welcome quite broad interpretations and feel that this latitude contributes to the music.

Although we cannot know exactly how Bach played, or wished his music to be played, we can find out a great deal about the conventions of his time, the way musical words and symbols were used, and thus get close enough to the composer's intention so that more of the "affect" and meaning of the music can come through to us in performance today. There is a large amount of source material available from the 16th, 17th, and 18th centuries. In fact, there is so much that it is necessary to limit it in a strategic manner when speaking about the music of J.S. Bach. We hope to be able to do this by examining information from a number of people who had differing kinds of relationships to Bach.

Johann Mattheson (1681-1764) was an organist, singer and composer from northern Germany. We can be quite sure that he knew Bach personally. Bach was one of a number of organists from whom Mattheson solicited a biography. (Bach never sent it!) He wrote two large works about performance: *Grosse General-Bass Schule* (1731) and *Der Voll-kommene Kapellmeister* (1739). Several themes by Bach are quoted in Mattheson's *Grosse General-Bass Schule,* in which he mentions Bach,

Händel, Telemann, Pachelbel, Praetorius, Schütz and many other musicians, some of whom are remembered today, many of whom are not. These works provide us with a great deal of information about "old style" Baroque performance practice in Germany, that is, a Baroque style which had not yet gone through transformation to become the later styles of Rococco ("galant") and Empfindsamkeit.

J. P. Kirnberger (1721-1783) was a close friend and student of Bach. He copied some of Bach's music and worked out realizations of the figured bass line of the third movement of the *Trio Sonata* from the *Musical Offering*. Bach evidently corrected these himself. He wrote several pedagogical works which obviously reflect Bach's teaching in combination with a newer style. In his time he was considered to be astute and penetrating, and an important figure in musical performance.

Johann Joachim Quantz (1697-1773) probably knew Bach and certainly heard him play. He wrote a treatise on playing the flute, *Versuch einer anweisung die Flöte traversiere zu spielen,* in which he speaks of Bach's playing with great enthusiasm. Musicologists today often state that he was talking about a performance style different from that of Bach. But Quantz was very cosmopolitan, and though I think that he was indeed speaking about an emerging style of composition, he was very much rooted in Baroque performance practice. We can often see whether he is talking about "old style" or "new style" by looking at certain clues he gives us. Often, these clues are in his use of tempo words. For instance, when he uses the word "affettuoso," we can assume he is talking about the "newer" style, as this term is rarely used by Bach and seldom found in older Baroque repertoire. (Bach uses this term in the second movement of the *Fifth Brandenburg Concerto*.) His treatise straddles both types of performance practice of his day: the Baroque and the "galant," and amalgamates certain qualities from both of them. Thus, in using Quantz as a source, we must be aware that he has one foot in each of these periods. In my opinion, these three authors are the most important sources for the music of J.S. Bach.

It is important to realize that in the latter part of Bach's life, both the "old" and the "new" styles were in vogue in various times and places. The "galant" style started in France in the early 1700's and became the later French Baroque style. This combination of styles did not die out until after the French Revolution in the 1790's. The Baroque in Germany and Austria died out sooner. So in studying source materials, it is important to relate the particular source to Bach's work not only chronologically, but also nationally. The two great styles of the time were the Italian style and the French style. The amalgamation of the two became the "German" style. These two styles are discussed in detail on p. 12 . The following authors, Mozart and North, are helpful, but of less weight than those mentioned previously.

Leopold Mozart (1719-1787) was both a composer and violinist. As a composer he is definitely associated with the "new style" and is not a part of the Baroque tradition in which Bach was writing. As an early Classical theorist he was, of course, thoroughly trained in Baroque style and knew it well. He sometimes ridicules the "old style." Both styles are shown in his treatise on violin-playing.

Roger North *(Roger North on Music,* ca. 1728), English theorist and composer, a follower of Corelli, wrote in great detail about performance practice.

There are others whose writings throw a helpful light on the study of source material in general:

J. G. Walther, a friend of Bach, wrote a *Musikalisches Lexikon* (1732); his work is mentioned by Mattheson.

Brossard was a French author who wrote a musical dictionary (1703).

Georg Muffat (1653-1704) was Kapellmeister in Passau in 1702, and his work, *Apparatus musico-organicus,* is cited by Mattheson. Muffat studied in France with Lully. [Jean Baptiste Lully (1632-1687) was an Italian who moved to France and became a naturalized citizen. Not much is known about his early life. However, through immense ambition and skilled use of intrigue, he came into complete control of music in France under Louis XIV.] In a work entitled *Florilegium Secundum,* 1698, Muffat codified Lully's teaching and techniques regarding orchestral playing, bowing, ornamentation and inequality. This text is especially helpful in considering the performance of the orchestral suites and other overture textures of Bach. This work was published in Augsburg in four different languages, and is a very good description of performance practice in the French style.

François Couperin (1668-1733) wrote a great deal about performance practice in the introduction to his first book of harpsichord works published in 1713, and in his *l'Art de Toucher le Clavecin,* 1717. He was the greatest composer of harpsichord music in the French Baroque period, and was quite explicit about the way in which he wanted his works to be performed. Bach copied one of Couperin's works into a notebook which he compiled for the Anna Magdalena Bach notebook.

Nicholas de Grigny, ca. 1699, published a *Livre d'Orgue* which Bach copied in his own hand.

We can also find information about Bach by looking at the music of his sons. **Wilhelm Friedemann Bach** (1710-1784), his eldest son, was a reclusive person, not well adapted to his times. (He composed in the "old" style.) It was for him that J.S. Bach wrote the pedal-clavier trio sonatas.

He traveled with his father a good deal and was present during the famous trip to the court of Frederick the Great in 1747, after which the *Musical Offering* was composed. The music of W.F. Bach shows many similarities to that of his father, including a predilection to writing in a fugal style. As we will see later, this son's use of numerology as a compositional tool gives us information about J.S. Bach's methods of composition, as this technique was certainly transmitted to him by his father (see p. 152).

There are others who were close to Bach who can be studied for clues about some of Bach's techniques of composition. **J.L. Krebs** (1713-1780) and **Lorenz Mizler** speak of Bach's scientific or mathematical manner of composition. Mizler tells us that the fourteenth fugue of *The Art of Fugue* was to have been followed by another fugue, invertible in all four parts. We know that Bach joined Mizler's society, a group of scientists and artists, and wrote the *Vom Himmel hoch* variations as a test piece for entrance into the society. We can thus assume that Mizler was quite knowledgeable about the esoteric secrets of Bach's manner of composition.

C.P.E. Bach (1714-1788), another of Bach's sons, is not a necessarily reliable source for our purposes. It appears that he was not very close to his father, and was certainly not close to the style of his father. J.S. Bach once said (as quoted to us by W.F. Bach) that this son's music "faded like Prussian blue" — not exactly a warm or accepting comment. One must ascertain whether C.P.E. Bach is speaking of his own musical style, or of the traditional Baroque style.

Other important but less strategic sources (because of date, nationality, stylistic influences) would include **Loulié** (ca. 1696), **Dom Bedos** (1709-1799), **Sancta Maria** (d. 1570), **Frescobaldi** (1583-1643) and **Diruta** (b. 1561). These and other sources will be mentioned only as corroborations of performance practice.

Sometimes it is possible to draw conclusions directly from the compositions themselves. This, of course, can put us on dangerous musicological ground. But drawing this type of conclusion is not only unavoidable, it is essential. No one ever performs a piece of music without drawing conclusions and putting them into practice. This makes it all the more important to distinguish between (a) conclusions that are objectively evident from the piece, about the piece, or from our knowledge of its place in musical history; (b) conclusions that are not conclusions at all, but personal projections onto a piece; and (c) the large grey area in between these two extremes. There is a relatively small amount of information which can be gathered from *any* source in relation to someone like J.S. Bach, since Bach himself wrote no performance-practice treatise; consequently we must be always vigilant about our manner of drawing conclusions, and about the kind of faith we invest in the conclusions we draw.

With this in mind, let us consider some examples of the kinds of deductions we can draw from specific pieces.

Example 5: Fantasia in G Major, S. 572 (Pièce d'Orgue)

This piece has French titles and a very simple pedal part that descends to a low B. We can reasonably place this work as a youthful work of Bach, probably written when he was visiting the French influenced court in Celle. Because the pedal part descends below C, we can infer that it was written for a French organ with ravalement, i.e., an extension beyond the usual compass, since French organs often descended to contra A, though German organs did not. We can also deduce that it was written for a friend or student of Bach, perhaps a Frenchman who did not play the pedals very well, as the pedal part is simple. French Baroque pedal-writing was *always* simple. (The obbligato pedal style was a north German invention and during the 17th and 18th centuries was limited to that area.) As a "French" work, it should be played with eighth note inequality. This is an example of the kind of deduction that can reasonably be made by simply looking at the piece itself.

The organ *Fantasia* and unfinished *Fugue in C Minor,* S. 562, is another example of a piece from which we can draw direct inferences:

Example 6: Fantasia and Fugue in C Minor, S. 562

We see that this fantasia is a five-voice fugue, with two voices in each hand, plus a simple pedal part. Bach studied the *Livre d'Orgue* of Nicholas de Grigny, copying the work in his own hand. This work contains a number of five-voice fugues, written with two voices in each hand, plus a very simple pedal part. Since the piece cited above is the *only* work in which Bach divided the fugal texture in this way, we can assume that the piece was modeled after the fugal textures of de Grigny. It is also written in larger note values (eighth notes), a further indication that it is patterned after de Grigny's style. Also, since the de Grigny fugues are traditionally registered for Cornet and a Cromorne in the manuals with a Flute pedal registration, we can draw the conclusion that this was the sound ideal which Bach had in mind when composing it. Thus we can determine the registration accordingly.

National Styles

In our attempt to use sources strategically, it is important to consider the two distinct national styles that influenced Bach: the French and the Italian.

The French school of keyboard music began in the 17th century when composers who wrote for the keyboard imitated music which was written for the lute. From this starting point there developed a unique school or style of writing, at least for the harpsichord. Later, an additional keyboard tradition grew out of using the cantus firmus technique as its basis. This style was mainly employed in organ composition. In addition to these techniques or styles, a French suite style, using various dance movements, was also developed. Other instruments as well as the harpsichord were used for the suites. There were very explicit methods of ornamental realization for all French Baroque music from its beginnings, ca. 1600. It is important to distinguish here between "ornaments," which were indicated by specific signs, and "embellishments," which were notes added by the performer to simpler note patterns. The two terms are often used interchangeably. (see p. 128), *Realization of Ornaments,* and p. 126, *Embellishments.)* In the French style ornamental signs were by far the more important. There was little improvisation of cadenzas, and little bravura ("brilliant") writing, i.e., constant 16th- or 8th-note motion in the music.

François Couperin specified that all his ornamental signs were to be strictly observed, but in his *Première Ordre* (1713) he also gave alternate embellishments which the performer could choose.

Example 7: François Couperin: Première Courante

* *Dessus plus orné sans changer la Basse.*   (the upper part is more ornate without changing
Voir Préface   the bass)

    The Italian style developed from a long tradition of vocal and later, instrumental composition, with a much stronger emphasis on bravura writing. Italian music, unlike French, included long chains of fast notes. This was especially true in violin and operatic music. The cadenza, first introduced in vocal music in Italy, later became important in keyboard and indeed all instrumental music. Slow movements were embellished with the wildest elaborations imaginable. Compared to each other, the French tradition would be called controlled and methodical, the Italian florid and free. Each school had problems understanding the other's music. France and Italy each had their own rules for inequality and other rhythmic adjustments, but the French were more precise in their *descriptions.* Around 1700, Corelli's influence in French instrumental music became strong. Here is an example of Italianate embellishment from the oeuvre of Corelli.

Arcangelo Corelli, Violin Sonatas, Op. V, Rome, 1700, No. 1, with free ornamental elaborations (first half of 18th century) by Francesco Geminiani, printed by Sir John Hawkins, *A General History ... of Music,* London, 1776, ed. of 1875, II, pp. 904ff.

Examples 8 and 9: Arcangelo Corelli: Violin Sonata No. 1

Corelli

The German tradition arose from an amalgamation of French and Italian styles. Scheidt, Schütz, and Froberger, in the early 1600's were the first to introduce the Italian influence to Germany. Later, during the height of Lully's career and after 1660, the French influence spread through all of Europe. Many German musicians went to either Italy or France, or both, to study. It was not until the beginning of the 18th century that there was a consciousness of a "German style." Mattheson devotes many pages of the first part of his *Grosse General-Bass Schule* to a defense of the proposition that someone (he modestly mentioned himself), who had never been to either Italy or France, was indeed qualified to write and teach the subject of music.

Bach was somewhat more influenced by the Italian than by the French tradition. In the *Clavierübung,* Book II, he writes "Nach Französicher Art" (after the French manner), and "Nach Italienischen gusto" after the *Concerto in F,* which shows that he was not afraid to make a stylistic copy and sign it as such (courantes, gigues, ouvertures, etc.). We gather that he knew about the French conventions because of the time that he spent at the French court in Celle during his teens. In general, though, he seems to have been more influenced by Italian music. Bach transcribed for solo clavier or organ nine of the Vivaldi concerti. Many of his keyboard figurations are taken from Italian violin figures. It is important to understand that, unlike today, the composers of the time were themselves virtuosi and style-setters for their contemporaries. For Baroque music, the great performers were all Italian violinists—Matteis, Corelli, Vivaldi, Geminiani and Tartini. This is reflected in the brilliant violin writing which Bach admired and imitated in his keyboard and violin writing.

The only element of keyboard music which is idiomatically German is the chorale prelude. This tradition began with Scheidt, ca. 1620, was continued by Walther, Schein and Buxtehude, and, of course, culminated in Bach.

The following shows how the Largo from *Trio in C,* S. 1072 might have been embellished by an Italian performer, and by a French performer.

Example 10: Trio in C, S. 1072

Italian version:

French version:

Criteria for Effective Performance

It is sometimes taken for granted that, in comparison to performers today, Baroque musicians were technically limited. Perhaps this comes from a 20th century feeling regarding "progress" and the awareness that in other disciplines requiring highly developed neuromuscular coordination (athletics, for instance) technical achievements are reached today that would have been thought impossible a few hundred years ago. But it appears to me that Baroque performers must have played with skill equal to the technical development of today's best performers. (There were fewer of them because of the lack of conservatory systems.) The evidence for this lies in the virtuoso pieces themselves. Bach's most difficult pieces tax even the most secure players today. Though there were relatively few people capable of playing these difficult works during Bach's time, it cannot be doubted that these performances were greatly skilled, and sounded magnificent when played by leading players of the time.

Mattheson's descriptions of what was expected of a Kapellmeister (contrapuntal improvisation, for example) also show us what an exacting discipline was brought to bear on the achievement of technical and musical skills. He takes many things for granted that would cause many musicians today who consider themselves "trained" to wonder if they would even qualify to begin study.

We read in Couperin that playing well depended on having "good taste." Mattheson spoke sarcastically about those who said it was "almost impossible to make rules, under the pretext that it depends on good taste," quoting Rameau. He felt that this was an exhibition of their weakness. (Mattheson, DVK, p. 133) This is certainly not the only point on which our sources disagreed. Couperin also said that "the distance between Grammar and Rhetoric is great enough, but the distance between musical notation and the art of playing well is infinitely greater." He continues, "I need not fear that enlightened performers will misunderstand me, but I must urge the others to be docile and to lay aside any prejudices they may have."

In another place, he said that what one sees on the page is often different from what one should hear, comparing this to the difference between the look of written French as it is spelled, and the sound of the language. This would seem to indicate a clear and widespread acceptance of a "performance understanding" of written musical notation that would make the "exactly as written" school of thought seem very strange to him.

Symbols for notes (pitches) on the staves are not ambiguous or imprecise, so it is the symbolism for dynamics and especially the relationships of the notes in time that present the problems for the performer to attempt to solve. The way that music is timed is of paramount importance, not only in the music of this period, but probably within any style. It is primarily the way the music falls within time that suggests to someone whether the performance is "correct" or "incorrect," effective or ineffective. The dynamic "correctness" of individual notes would be next in importance, even though dynamic changes on individual notes are not possible on the harpsichord or organ, except by suggestion through articulation and time devices.

In addition to general questions of timing, these are some of the other factors that a performer must consider in the attempt to find the optimal energy level for any composition:

- the sound of the instrument (dynamics, timbre and range)
- the environment of the sound (the room—there were no large concert halls; concerts with large forces were held in churches)
- the articulation
- the rubato
- the additions to the text of the music.

There is little discussion in the sources from Bach's time about the first two points, but there are detailed discussions of the other three, as well as of the broader questions of timing and rhythm already mentioned. Mattheson says that "a good mediation [perhaps we can understand 'fluctuation' or even 'give-and-take'] of the tempo" (GGBS, p. 195) is what makes a bad piece sound good, or a good piece sound bad.

If all these factors are considered, the chances for the original energy of the piece to emerge in performance are greatly improved.

Meters, Tempi and Accents
. . . a general introduction

Basic to all questions of rhythm in Baroque music is the concept of alternations between "strong" and "weak," not only as applied to individual notes, but extending to many different structural levels of music. (see p. 63) for specific discussion of how to determine where strong and weak notes, beats or measures occur, and for suggestions of what this means in performance.) This concept was taken for granted in all European music as far back as the 16th century. The Italians referred to *"note buone"* and *"note cattive"* ("good" and "bad" notes), or in Latin to *"nobilis"* and *"vilis."* These were also referred to as "principal notes" or "passing notes." This concept of strong/weak alternation underlies most of the specific considerations that follow: meters, accents, fingering, rubato, etc.

The symbols – and ᵕ which today we know principally in connection with the scansion of poetry, e.g., the curfew tolls the knell of parting day, were known and accepted in musical notation. Some of the sources state quite clearly that they believe this concept of strong/weak alternation in music originated in poetry, in the natural tendency of spoken language to fall into patterns of stressed and unstressed syllables. Others find correlations in dance movements, in fact, with all the polarities of life, including, of course, the natural strong-weak pulse of the heartbeat. Mattheson says that the main characteristic of meter is that it falls into *two* parts which "take their origin from the arteries whose up and down beats are called, by those who understand medicine, 'sistolic' and 'diastolic.' "

In spoken poetry, strong/weak are indicated by alterations of both volume and duration. Depending on the possibilities of each musical instrument, strong/weak patterns were indicated by alterations in either or both of these. (The symbols ⌐ and ᵥ , used by string players to indicate bowing, probably derive from the Latin words **"n**obilis*" and "***v**ilis").* Because the organ and harpsichord have no potential for dynamic alteration, the rhythmic alterations are of even greater importance.

It was taken for granted that a piece should rarely, if ever, be performed at a mechanically precise tempo from start to finish. Mattheson said:

> . . . a row of tones which are perceived hastily and following one upon another affect the ear quite differently than if the same tones are presented slowly with good mediation [not only] of the tempo itself, but of the on-

the-beat [good] notes ["*anschlagende Noten*"] in particular, and their relative importance. This tempo makes that which appears bad to be good, and that which appears good to be bad, depending on whether it is arranged short or long, fast or slow.

(Grosse General-Bass Schule, p. 195)*

Frescobaldi spoke of music being governed by "a changing beat . . . not subject to strict time . . . the bulk of notes to be taken in proper proportion . . . the beat being left to the good taste of the player" *(Toccatae,* 1617). Similar passages from different national styles, over a period of several hundred years could be cited. When Mattheson speaks about "mediation of the tempo" and of the "relative importance" of notes within the tempo, he is talking about the general framework of rhythmic alteration that is basic to our understanding of the performance of the music of his time. Roger North refers to chains of fast notes with no accents as "fidle fadle." One must, however, exercise more freedoms in pieces like toccatas, fantasias, and preludes, and less in stricter styles, i.e., fugues.

In 1856 Franz Liszt referred in a letter to a "mode of playing, still customary in some places . . . a mechanical kind of playing which, *meticulously adhering to the meter, splits up the performance by perpetually emphasizing the strong and weak beats.*" He stated that he did not wish this kind of rhythmic convention to be applied to his compositions, but preferred "only that kind of periodic style of execution which emphasizes the essential accents and displays the nuances of the music by means of melodic and rhythmic shaping." It is somewhat amusing to picture the conscientious, old-fashioned musicians to whom he referred, trying to apply the conceptions of strong/weak structural fluctuations in which they were trained to the "modern music" of their day. Perhaps if Bach saw *us* trying to play *his* music without a knowledge of these conventions, he would be equally amused.

These alterations within the tempo were absolutely essential in conveying the inner meaning of the music. The performer learned to recognize the strong/weak structures, important stressed beats, and deviations from the rhythmic norm. The musician's problem of applying this kind of insight to performance is similar to the task of the actor reading Shakespeare. The true meaning of the music could never be conveyed in strict time, especially on instruments with no possibilities for dynamic gradations, such as the organ and the harpsichord.

Because it is difficult to talk precisely about playing imprecisely, verbal descriptions of rhythmic alterations lead to wide differences and misunderstandings of taste and opinion. One performer's lengthening of notes might strike one listener as subtly delightful, while it may cause another to feel that enormous distortions of the beat are taking place, and leave yet another to feel that the general effect is still far too mechanical.

•   •   •

From the time of Frescobaldi through Bach, it was commonly understood that each metric signature had a specific accent pattern as well as an inherent tempo. This was a part of notational tradition and it is talked about in a great many sources. It would be convenient if we could come right out and state that Bach knew all these conventions and used them. In place of a direct statement from Bach, we will rely on Kirnberger [*Kunst des reinen Sätzes in der Music,* Berlin, 1774, Book II, part IV, pp. 105-153] to provide us with a good deal of information on his teacher's (J.S. Bach) usage of time signatures and Italian tempo words, and then fill in the rest of the information with sources quoted previously.

One of the problems we have with Bach's works is that many of them have come down to us via copies made by other people who were unaware of the time signature conventions, or who were careless about them. This is especially true of the use of the symbols for common time, C, and for cut time, ₵. These were often copied interchangeably. However, properly understood, they designated different beat and speed patterns. We even find that at a certain time engravers substituted C for ₵ at will, depending on whether or not they had a ₵ as part of their typeset. This has resulted in a serious misunderstanding of musical intentions regarding tempo and beat pattern in a number of pieces. When we are dealing with manuscript copies, we have to determine whether it is Bach's own copy, that of a student who had been faithful to Bach's understanding of the conventions, or that of a stranger or foreigner who might not have understood the accepted practice. The same would, of course, apply to all periods of music.

We know that Mattheson thought it was important to differentiate between seemingly similar time signatures. Replying to those who accused him of adding needlessly obscure signs, he said,

> The signatures 2/4, 2/8 and 2 [or ₵] are not in the least bit obscure, but are very simple and natural, and those people who think one could simply write a C in their stead are in error, have no experience, and don't know how to write time signatures. (GGBS, p. 375)

If we find a manuscript using a ₵, we can usually assume it to be correct as the more frequent error in the older manuscripts was to write C where ₵ was originally intended. On the other hand, however, we have an interesting exception with the *D Minor Harpsichord Concerto,* S. 1052. There are two important copies of this piece, one having a C, or common time, and one having ₵, or cut time, with an "Allegro" designation. There is also an organ version of the first movement *(Cantata 146)* in common time with no Italian qualifying word. In this case, because we have the organ version marked C, I would tend to feel that all versions should in fact be "played" in common time, since two out of three use the common time signature. The concerto is also quoted in "C" by Kirnberger.

We also have to understand that Bach sometimes changed his mind about time signatures. This did not happen very often, but there are a few examples. The two forms of the 17 "verschiedene Choralen," (varied Chorales) the earlier one called the *Weimarer Fassung* (Weimar Version) and the later one called the *Leipziger Fassung* (Leipzig Version), each contain three settings of "Nun komm der Heiden Heiland." In the *Weimar version* the second setting is in cut time, and the third in common time (see examples 11 and 12), but in the *Leipzig Version* the second setting is in common time, and the third setting in cut time with eighth notes (See examples 11a and 12a). As we will see later, eighth notes in ₵ had the same intrinsic value as sixteenth notes in C; the reason for the different signature was to indicate a different pattern of accents. The fact that Bach's idea of accents and tempo changed is also demonstrated in the two versions of "Herr Jesu Christ dich zu uns wend" from the 17 "verschiedene Choralen," the earlier version of which is in ₵ and the later in C. (See examples 13 and 13a)

Example 11: Nun komm, der Heiden Heiland, S. 660a
Weimarer Fassung, second setting in ₵

Example 11a: Nun komm, der Heiden Heiland, S. 660
Leipziger Fassung, second setting in C

Example 12: Nun komm, der Heiden Heiland, S. 661a
Weimarer Fassung, third setting in C in sixteenth notes

Example 12a: Nun komm, der Heiden Heiland, S. 661
Leipziger Fassung, third setting in ₵ in eighth notes

Example 13: Herr Jesu Christ, dich zu uns wend, S. 665
Weimarer Fassung in ₵

Example 13a: Herr Jesu Christ, dich zu uns wend, S. 655a
Leipziger Fassung in C

Other time signature changes occur in differing versions of the B minor
Prelude, WTC II, and parts of the *Art of Fugue*.

Tactus ... Pulse, Beat and Time Signatures

Tactus, sometimes called pulse or beat, is a basic rhythmic concept that stems from the Renaissance. Tactus can be defined as a normal, recurring beat or pulse which remains constant. If we say that a piece of music is "fast" or slow," we are presuming that there is some kind of "normal" tempo against which fast and slow tempi can be measured. This so-called normal tempo is the tactus, which, when measured on the metronome (an invention of the early 19th century), falls somewhere between 60 and 80, the average being usually about 72. This figure corresponds to the average human heartbeat. The "Renaissance" tactus is probably slightly slower, perhaps about 60.

It is of interest to note that in elaborate Renaissance vocal music the tactus must be either 60, for duple meter, or 80, for triple meter. The reason we can know this with such certainty is that there is a certain laryngeal technique for producing a rapid series of notes which will only work at one speed, with only the slightest variation for individual differences. This is sometimes called the "trillo technique," or the "chuckle technique." The intrinsic value of the notes produced in this way is always the same. When they fall into groups of 8, the tactus is 60, and when they fall into groups of 6, the tactus is 80.

Originally, this technique was used to produce a series of rapid notes on one tone, as in the "goat bleat" (used in ornamentation of Monteverdi), later it was then used to produce the rapid series of notes codified in the standard works on vocal ornamentation of the 16th and 17th centuries. (I am grateful to Alden Gilchrist for this information.)

So, when our sources are discussing tempi relative to the concept of "tactus" or pulse, they are giving us quite precise information which is not difficult to understand. Although sources vary considerably about time signature designations, I think it is possible to get a clear picture of what the words and symbols meant to Bach and his contemporaries.

Here are some excerpts from Kirnberger [my comments in brackets]:

Anyone can see at first glance that the most moving song would be robbed of all power and expression if one note were performed after the other according to no particular rules of speed, without accents and without pauses, even if the tones were played with the most precise purity. (*Die Kunst des...*, p. 105, line 5 ff.)

Therefore it is movement, beat and rhythm which give to a song its life and its power . . . (line 17, ff.)

Every piece of dance music has its particular "beat movement" [Taktbewegung] which is determined by the meter and by the note values which are used within it. With regard to meter, those with longer beats, such as the alla breve, 3/2 and 6/4, move more heavily and slowly than those with shorter beats, such as the 2/4, 3/4 and 6/8, and these in turn are less lively than the 3/8 and 6/16. Thus, for example, a Loure in 3/2 has a slower beat movement than a minuet in 3/4, and this in turn is slower than a passepied in 3/8. With regard to note values, dance pieces using 16ths and 32nds as the fastest note value have a slower beat movement than those using primarily 8ths with a few 16ths. Thus, for example, a Sarabande in 3/4 has a slower beat movement than a minuet, even though they may both be written in the same meter. [In general, then, the larger the denominator of the signature, the faster the tempo.] (p. 106, line 28 ff., through p. 107, line 12)

Thus, the *tempo giusto is determined by the meter and by the length or shortness of the note values in a piece.* If the young composer gets a proper feeling for this, then he will soon recognize how the natural tempo of a piece gains or loses in speed or slowness by the addition of the qualifying words largo, adagio, andante, allegro, presto, and their modifications, such as larghetto, andantino, allegretto, or prestissimo. [Here Kirnberger gives us the influencing Italian words in order of acceleration.] (p. 106, line 28 ff., through p. 107, line 12)

Finally, the composer must not forget to indicate as precisely as possible the proper movement of his piece to the extent that it is not already determined by the above named characteristics. He must use the words allegro assai, allegro moderato, poco allegro, etc., wherever the word allegro alone would make the tempo too fast or not fast enough; with slower pieces, the same would apply. The words which describe the characteristic movement, such as maestoso, scherzando, vivo, mesto, etc., are often of utmost importance and not to be treated lightly by one who wishes to perform the piece well. (p. 112, line 28 ff.)

It is exactly as with common speech, in which it is only through the use of accents and the length or shortness of syllables that we can make words and phrases distinguishable.

Meter consists of the exact uniformity of accents which are put onto a few tones, and in the completely regular distribution of long and short syllables. It is when these particular heavy or light accents re-occur on the same beats that a song receives its meter or beat. If these accents were not distributed regularly, creating the exact periodic repetition, then the song would resemble very common prose speech; through these periodic repetitions, however, it resembles verse which has its exact meter. (p. 113, line 23)

[Speaking of the 2/1 meter] Instead of it one should rather use 2/2 or 6/4 with the qualifying word "grave" in order to describe the emphatic and heavy performance that this meter demands. In the works of the older Bach, I know of only one Credo *(Mass in B minor)* in the big alla breve meter with two semibreves; however, he describes this with ₵ in order to show that the rests have the same value as in the ordinary alla-breve meter. (p. 118, line 8 ff; line 13)

[About 2/2 or ₵, or allabreve] It is to be noted that this meter is very heavy and emphatic, but still it is to be performed at a speed indicated by the note values, unless the qualifying words grave, adagio, etc., specify a slower tempo. The same is true of the related 6/4 meter, of two triple beats, but the tempo giusto of this meter is somewhat more moderate. No note values smaller than 8ths may be used. [Four 8ths in ₵ would then equal the beat.] (p. 118, line 18 ff.)

The 2/4 meter has the same movement as the allabreve, but is performed far more lightly. [I would infer "faster" also.] This difference between the performance of the two meters is so palpable that one could not possibly suppose it to be unimportant whether a piece is written in ₵ or in 2/4. (p. 118, line 18 ff.)

J.S. Bach and Couperin had their reasons when they wrote some of their pieces in 6/16. Who does not know the Bach fugue WTC II, *Fugue in F Major?* (p. 119, line 18 ff.)

Example 14: Well Tempered Clavier, Book II: Fugue in F Major, S. 880

If it is rewritten into 6/8, the movement is no longer the same, the pace is far heavier, the notes, at least the held ones, receive too much weight, in short, the expression of the whole piece suffers and is no longer the same as Bach put into it. [6/16 is lighter and faster than 6/8] (p. 120)

If this fugue is to be properly performed on the keyboard, the notes must be played with a light, fleeting movement without the slightest pressure; this is what the 6/16 notes indicate. On the violin pieces in this and similar meters are to be performed only with the tip of the bow, but pieces in the heavier meters require a longer stroke and more pressure on the bow. (p. 120)

This must be said about these meters with two beats, that each measure consists of a foot with two parts, the first long and the second short, and that therefore the main note of a melody must fall on the first beat of the measure, as it is called, on the down beat. [Kirnberger calls our attention to the differences between strong and weak beats in a measure, and the strength of the down beat.] (p. 120, line 17)

The 4/2 meter, or $\mathbb{O}$, like the 2/1 meter, is no longer in use, and because of the disorder caused in this meter by rests, it is to be avoided. The same is true of the 12/4 meter with four triple beats, which is derived from it. (p. 122, line 11 ff.)

The 4/4 meter, indicated by C, is of two kinds. It can be used instead of the 4/2 meter, just described, using the qualifying word grave, and is then called the "great 4/4 meter," or it is the so-called common even meter, also called the "little 4/4 meter."

The great 4/4 has an extremely heavy movement and expression, and because of its emphatic nature is used primarily in large pieces of church music, choruses and fugues; 8ths and a few groups of 16ths are its fastest note values. In order to distinguish it from the little 4/4, one should notate it with 4/4 instead of with C. These two meters have nothing in common with each other except their marking.

The little 4/4 has a more lively movement and is to be performed with far more lightness. It can use all note values up to 16ths and can be used in the most varied ways for all kinds of compositions.

The 12/8 meter with triple beats which is derived from the 4/4 has similar characteristics. Some of the older composers who were very particular about the performance of their compositions often used the marking 24/16 on pieces in 12/8 with mainly 16th notes, in order to indicate that the 16ths should be played *lightly* and *hastily* without the slightest pressure on the first note of each beat. These subtleties seem to be so unknown to today's composers and performers that they believe these meter markings to have been idiosyncracies of the old composers.

Of the meters in 4, the 4/8 is the lightest in presentation and movement. It differs from 2/4 in that the weight on each beat is even, whereas in 2/4 the first and third are accented. [Kirnberger shows in his example that 4/8 = strong, weak, weak, weak; whereas 2/4 = strong, nothing, weak, nothing.] (p. 122, line 30 through p. 123, line 22)

In the meters in 4, the first and third are long, also called "good beats," and the second and fourth are short, also called "bad beats." The first is heavier than the third. (line 8 ff.)

3/1 is replaced by the two following meters, especially when the qualifying word *Grave* is added to them. (page 127, line 5)

3/2 is often used in church music because of the heavy and slow performance indicated by its note values. In church music its smallest note values are quarter notes, very occasionally 8ths. In chamber music 16ths can also be used. C.P.E. Bach even used this meter for a sinfonia which begins with many 32nd notes in succession. (line 9 ff.)

Even though 3/2 (♩ ♩ ♩) and 6/4 (♩.♩.) each contain six quarter notes, these two meters do not resemble each other, because of the difference of the weight on each beat. Still, it is of particular interest that old, good composers treated the Courante, which is usually set in 3/2, in such a way that the two meters are often confused with each other. For example, the first part of a *Courante for Clavier* by Couperin (see p. 13), the second and sixth measures, and the bass melody of the seventh measure of this Courante are in 3/2, but the other measures are in 6/4. In J.S. Bach's works one finds a great many Courantes treated in this way. (line 18, ff., through p. 128, line 4)

The 3/4 meter is not found in church music as often as the 3/2, because it is to be performed more lightly, but it is found in the most varied uses in chamber and theater music.

Its natural movement is that of a minuet and as such it cannot use too many 16ths in succession, and even less so, 32nds. (p. 129, line 4 to 9)

One errs if one considers this meter, 9/8, to be simply a 3/4 with triplets: anyone who is at all competent as a performer knows that triplets in 3/4 must be played differently from 8ths in 9/8. The former are played very lightly without the slightest pressure on the last note, but the latter are played more heavily and with some weight on the last note. The former can never, or only seldom, accept a harmony on the last note, but the latter quite often. The former can accept no break in the 16ths, but the latter can easily do so. If both meters were not clearly different from each other, then all Gigues in 6/8 could just as well have been written in 2/4, 12/8 would be the same as C, and 6/8 the same as 2/4; anyone can easily see how senseless this would be by simply trying to put a Gigue into 12/8, or a 6/8 into C or 2/4.

The older composers used 18/16 with three triple beats when they wanted to indicate that the piece was to be performed lightly, fleetingly and without the slightest pressure on the first note of each beat.

But since such subtleties of performance have been lost, so that many who are called virtuosi perform six 16ths as if they were two groups of triplets, then the 18/16 meter belongs to those lost meters that we can easily do without. (p. 129, line 13)

The 3/8 meter has the lively movement of a Passepied; it is to be performed lightly, but not frivolously, and is used extensively in chamber and theater music.

The 9/16 meter with 3 triple beats, which derives from the 3/8, was often used by the older composers for gigue-like pieces which were to be performed with extremely lively and light movement; in today's music, however, it is no longer used. The 9/8 takes its place. [J. S. Bach occasionally uses this signature, i.e., the Gigue from *Partita 4 in D* for harpsichord.] (p. 130, line 7)

When 8ths are used in 3/4 meters, and 16ths in 3/8, then the first note of each group is long. [This would indicate holding the note slightly.]

(Comments on the "set-together" meters)

In even meters with two beats, and in triple meters, there are melodies in which it is clear that entire measures are alternately heavy and light, so that one feels an entire measure to consist of one beat. When the melody is so constructed that one feels the entire measure to be a single beat, then two measures must necessarily be set together to make a single one, with the first part being long and the second part short.

For if this setting-together did not occur, one would have a melody consisting only of heavy beats because of the necessary heaviness of the down beat. This would be just as offensive as a portion of speech which consisted only of words of one syllable, each of them accented. [This is a brilliant setting forth and justification of strong and weak measure construction.] (p. 131, line 20)

This is the origin of the set-together meters, that is, the 4/4 which is put together from two single measures of 2/4, or the 6/8 which is put together from two single measures of 3/8, and so forth.

Actually, this setting-together only occurs so that the player can find the correct mode of performance and can play the second half of such a measure more lightly than the first. One can easily distinguish these meters from the others; for instance, the set-together 4/4 from the single common 4/4, in that the ending in the set-together ones fall quite naturally on the second half of the measure and only last for half a measure, whereas in common 4/4 this would not be at all possible. In the same way, the endings in the set-together 6/4 can fall on the fourth quarter, which would be quite impossible in single 6/4. [A great many Bach works have cadences on the second part of a 4/4 measure, i.e., *C Major Fugue*, WTC I. We can assume, then, that they are written in this "set-together" manner.]

[Perhaps the "set-together" measure idea comes from the compositional need to have other than two measure groupings, e.g., three measure groupings. The 4/4, reduced into measures of 2/4, would allow a grouping of three measures of 2/4 to be easily perceived. This is proved in 4/4 time when the cadence falls on the second half of the measure where, in fact, we have a grouping of three 2/4 (or the "set-together" type) measures.]

It is to be stated generally about the meters which contain the same numbers of beats, the one that has larger or longer measure subdivisions is naturally more serious than the one with shorter parts. Thus the 4/4 meter is less cheerful than the 4/8; the 3/2 is heavier than the 3/4, which in turn is not so light as the 3/8.

For ceremonial and emotionally heavy ("pathetisch") pieces, the allabreve meter is ideal and is therefore used in motets and other ceremonial church pieces. The great 4/4 has a very emphatic and serious pace and is appropriate for marvelous choruses, fugues in church pieces, and generally in all pieces calling for majesty and seriousness. The 3/2 is heavy and extremely serious if there are not too many small-note values used in it.

For a lively and wakeful expression which, however, still has something emphatic about it, the 4/4 is best. The 2/4 is also lively, but is already associable with more lightness and can thus be used for more frivolous pieces. The 4/8 moves quite fleetingly and its liveliness has nothing more to do with the emphatic nature of 4/4. Gentle and noble is the character of the 3/4, especially when it consists solely or mainly of quarter notes. The 3/8 is of a cheerfulness which verges on the audacious. (p. 133, line 12 ff.)

From Kirnberger's statement we can certainly deduce that each signature has its own specific accent pattern, tempo character, and mood —and that the added Italian (sometimes French) words change the meaning of the signature in some way. Using Kirnberger, Quantz, Mattheson and other corroborating sources, we can arrive at the following information about signatures.

In speaking about the following time signatures it should be noted that the terms "beat," "tactus" or "pulse" are not to be confused with the terms "accent" or "accents per measure."

Common time (C) is four beats per measure; the first and the third are strong, the second and fourth are weak. The strong beats are accented by holding the note slightly, the hold varying from almost imperceptible to noticeable. This holding of the first and third counts is corroborated by Loulié and Kirnberger. The weak beats are passed through with no accent. Strong beats are also slightly louder than weak beats in instruments that allow for dynamic variation. (For descriptions of the conventions regarding strong and weak beats/measures, etc.,   (see p. 19.) Down beats, or the first beat after a bar line, are the strongest of all. The bar line, evolving as a general feature of music ca. 1610, gives the strongest clue to the placement of primary accents.

Note values within the C signature: One determines the number of notes per beat or tactus by determining the smallest note value which is not of an ornamental nature. Four of these smallest-note values (usually 8ths or 16ths) are equal to tactus, unless there is an Italian tempo-qualifying word. For instance:

Example 15: Fugue in F Sharp Major, WTC I, S. 858

In this example the 32nd notes are merely the end of a trill and would obviously be considered ornamental.   = T

Example 16: Fugue in D Major, WTC II, S. 874

In this example the occasional 16th-note motion would be considered ornamental.

Example 17: Invention 14, S. 785

The smallest non-ornamental note value is 16th notes, even though the 32nd note figures occur in great quantity. This example is less obvious than the previous two.

In a texture filled with 32nd notes with a common or even cut time signature, it is more difficult to determine the tempo, as sources do not describe four 32nd notes as being equal to the beat. More about that later. Within common time with sixteen 16th notes in a measure, the first and the ninth are accented:

Example 18

If the measure has four quarter notes as the fastest value, then these four are equal to tactus or the beat. Since the larger note value style of notation is of an older tradition, i.e., Renaissance, the tactus probably moves a bit more slowly, ca. 60:

Example 19

This style of large note values with one tactus per measure is sometimes called "a capella." The tradition of using larger note values comes from a more antique style and this notational convention was used by Bach when he chose to imitate this style. Some examples of this are the Credo from the *B Minor Mass* and the Kyries from the third part of the Clavierübung. The following examples have two accents per measure: the tactus = two quarters.

Example 20: B Minor Mass (Credo), S. 232

Example 21: Clavierübung III (Kyries), S. 699, 670, 671

Cut time (¢), according to some sources, is twice as fast as common time. But it is difficult to say whether the sources are talking about the intrinsic lengths of the notes as written or about the actual speed. If one is playing eighth notes in ¢, they in fact have the same intrinsic length as sixteenth notes in C, so this is a question of definition, not of interpreting the tempo. Some of the sources say that ¢ is somewhat faster than C. Quantz describes a "good allegro" by suggesting that it should have a beat equal to tactus and a half, which, translated to present metronome markings, would mean 90-120, with an average of about 108. So perhaps we can assign that tempo to ¢ with 16ths.

Note values within the ¢ signature: Cut time with 16th notes has two accents per measure, the first is a strong accent, and the second (on the ninth 16th note) is weak.

Example 22

If the piece is written in 8th notes in ¢, the first note of each measure is accented and there are no further accents:

Example 23

Cut time with only quarter notes occurs rarely. It is more usual to find cut time with quarter notes in a 4/2 signature. When quarter notes are the fastest value in cut time, they will have the same value as 8th notes in common time signatures. However, there will be only one measure for every four quarter notes, or one beat per measure. It is more common to see measures of 4/2 time with eight quarter notes as the basic motion.

The tempo of ¢ with eighth notes is the same as common time with 16ths. Cut time with eighths uses tactus for every four 8th notes; it does not speed up the tempo. The difference between cut time and common time in 8th notes is more a question of inequality (see p. 105) .

Example 24: Cantata 103, Opening Movement

This stunning example proves the relationship between C and ₵. The beginning of the fugue subject is written as quarter, eighth note in common time, and then as half, quarter note in the ensuing cut time.

Signatures in /4:

2/4 has one beat per measure and is generally considered a fast signature, which within our system means a tempo of tactus and a half (90-120, or an average of about 108 on the metronome):

Example 25

The *C Major Fugue* from the second book of the *Well Tempered Clavier* is an interesting example. It has three versions, including an earlier version in 4/4 time and a later version in 2/4. Bach evidently changed his mind about the tempo and accent patterns for the later version, and gave a new slant to it by making the piece longer, and speeding up the tempo, as 2/4 is naturally faster and lighter.

Example 26: C Major Fugue, S. 870a (early version):

Example 27: C Major Fugue, S. 870 (later version):

3/4 is generally referred to as a fast signature. Leopold Mozart called it "wild," i.e., the accent pattern is often irregular. Normally there is a strong accent on the first beat of a 3/4 measure, but Leopold Mozart, in his violin treatise (1756, p. 120-123), said that he had heard this signature accented in different ways: on the second or on the third beat, or quite irregularly. As we know, the hemiola (stressing a duple pattern in a triple meter) at the approach to cadences which is created by the stressing of unexpected beats, is very common in Baroque music.

Example 28: Concerto in D Minor for 3 harpsichords, S. 1063

Other kinds of rhythmic digressions from the norm also occur more frequently in 3/4 than in other signatures. Quantz suggests that to determine the proper tempo for 3/4, the performer should make two quarter notes equal to pulse, even if there are 16th notes intermingled. Quantz further said that the speed of tactus or pulse was 80 per minute. This means that he felt 3/4 should be played at a speed equivalent to today's metronome marking of 160 per quarter note, which must obviously be approximated somewhat, even at Quantz's own suggestion.

In general, triple meter (except for 3/2) is somewhat faster than duple, the tradition stemming from the Renaissance.

6/4 with 8th notes, has six 8th notes to a beat. There are two beats per measure, the second one (on the seventh 8th note) is weak:

Example 29:

Signatures in /8

3/8 with 16th notes is played at tactus for the measure; one accent usually occurs on the first 16th:

Example 30

beat pattern   tempo

= tactus

6/8 with 8th notes is played at tactus for the measure and has one accent on the first beat, which is, of course, strong. When we are dealing with time signatures having smaller denominators, the concept of strong and weak *measures* (not only strong and weak *beats*) becomes even more important than in time signatures with smaller denominators. The measures themselves are so small that there can be no more than one accent within them, so the performer must consider not only which beats, but which measures, are strong or weak:

Example 31

beat pattern   tempo

= tactus

6/8 with 16ths has the same tempo as the other triple, i.e., any multiple of three in the numerator, meters, i.e., tactus for every three 8th notes. Still, there is only one strong beat in 6/8, even with 16th notes, because the second, which would be expected to fall on the seventh 16th note, would not be accented in time, but would probably be slurred to the 8th or 16th note following it:

Example 32

beat pattern   tempo

= tactus

9/8 with 8th notes has two accents per measure. The first falls at the beginning of the first group of three notes and is strong. The second group of three notes has no beat accent at all, and the initial note of the third group of three receives an accent that is neither strong nor weak but somewhere in between. This accent pattern is demonstrated by the way

Bach and many Baroque composers write the typical accompaniment of
9/8:

This convention regarding 9/8 with 8th notes continued into the end of the 18th century and is last mentioned in G. Sulzer's *Der schönen Kunste* (1792). The tempo of 9/8 with 8th notes is determined by making six of the 8th notes, or ⅔ of each measure equal to tactus:

Example 33

beat pattern   tempo

= tactus

9/8 with 16th notes is played with six 16ths, or ⅓ of each measure equal to tactus:

Example 34

beat pattern
(can also be "wild," like 3/4)   tempo

= tactus

12/8 with a mixture of 8th and 16th notes has two strong structural beats which fall, as in common time, on the first and third beats of the measure. The tempo is three 8th notes for tactus:

Example 35

beat pattern   tempo

or

= tactus

12/8 with only 8th notes has one strong beat per measure. The accent on the beginning of the third group of 8th notes is slight, probably a slur. The tempo is six 8th notes equal to tactus:

Example 36

beat pattern   tempo

= tactus

Signatures in /16
Excepting Kirnberger and Mattheson, not many sources talk about

these signatures. 6/16 is like 6/8, with the note values halved and played faster, lighter, with hardly any accent or pressure.

9/16 is an unusual signature. Mattheson uses this signature on the thirteenth exercise in the advanced section of his *Grosse General-Bass Schule,* and qualifies it with "Con Spirito." He thought it was unusual enough that he made the following bizarre comment:

> Perhaps one could just as well have written this piece in 9/8 and simply written Allegro over it [thus proving its (9/16)greater speed, and that Allegro meant "faster" to Mattheson]; nonetheless it certainly can't hurt some of you who have never seen a 9/16 signature to see one, so we give it to you now to deal with so that if you should ever run across it at some other time, you will have the proper respect for it. . . . It is a great foolishness to use obscure signatures which will only make doubtful the meaning of a simple melody . . . but in order to express fast things, one must use a signature denoting a fast beat and fast notes, so that the symbols and the things themselves coincide. (Mattheson, GGBS, p. 374)

12/16 is the same as 12/8, but it is faster, lighter, and almost accentless.

24/16 is unusual. It is used in the *G Major Prelude* from the first book of the *Well Tempered Clavier:*

Example 37: Prelude in G Major, S. 860

When Bach writes large measures with many 16th notes, as he does in this piece, he wants a bravura effect with constant motion. The more notes there are per measure, the fewer opportunities there are for stopping or holding back. The reason is that there are fewer strong beats which would dictate holding back. Since the bottom voice of this example is in common time and the top voice in 24/16, the common time accent pattern is clearly understood to be two strong beats per measure, with each beat (or six 16th notes) equal to tactus + + . (We will use + signs to indicate a slightly faster beat or tactus.)

Signatures Commonly Used by Bach and His Contemporaries

Signature	Fastest note value	Accents	Source Tempo	Comments
C	16ths	1, 3	four 16ths = T	First and third beats held slightly; *K* suggests 4/4 instead of C
C	8ths	1, 3		Sources are not clear about this signature; I suggest T+ for a quarter, with a possibility of inequality treatment
¢	quarters	1		Using the "fastest-note value" technique, I suggest four quarters to a slow beat
¢, or 2	8ths	1	four 8ths = T	
	16ths	1 (3 is weak)	somewhat faster	I suggest four 16ths = T-½
𝄴, or ¢	Overture style includes 32nds	1, 3	slow, stately	I suggest a slow T to each quarter, but see section on Overture style
3/2	8ths	1, or in Sarabande 2	four 8ths = T, heavy	Inequality in Courante-type pieces, as well as irregular accents
3/2	16ths	1, but quite free		I suggest four 16ths = T-½
2/4	16ths	1	fast, lively	I suggest four 16ths = T-½
3/4	16ths	1, but irregular	fast, to very fast	I suggest four 16ths = T-½ or T-½+; *Q* calls for T x 2 in Allegro 3/4
3/4	8ths	1	each measure receives a beat	

Signature	Fastest-note value	Accents	Source Tempo	Comments
3/4	quarters	1	gentle, noble	I suggest a beat for each measure
6/4	8ths	1	$\downarrow$. = T	
3/8	16ths	1	light, Passe-pied tempo; six 16ths = T	
4/8	8ths with a few 16ths	1, with weak accent on 3	cheerful	I suggest four 16ths = T-½
6/8	16ths	1 (3)	six 16ths = T	
6/8	8ths	1	six 8ths = T	
9/8	16ths	1	six 16ths = T	
9/8	8ths	1, 3	six 8ths = T	
12/8	16ths	1,3	six 16ths = T	
12/8	8ths	1,3	six 8ths = T	
6/16	16ths	1	six 16ths = T	lighter and faster than 6/8
9/16	16ths	1, but irregular	six 16ths = T	lighter and faster than 9/8; no accent on third count as in 9/8 with 8ths
12/16 or 24/16	16ths	1, or 1, 3	six 16ths = T + (+)	lighter and faster than 12/8; 24/16 is brilliant and accentless

For the signatures more difficult to ascertain—₵ with 16ths, 3/4 with 16ths, and C with 8th notes—I have adopted the following solutions: ₵ with 16ths will go at T-½ (somewhat faster, the sources say); 3/4 with 16ths will go at T-½ + (Mozart says "fast," and Quantz suggests double pulse for the quarter in Allegro 3/4); C with 8th notes (the style of the French organ masses, which also features ₵ with 8th notes), I have adopted T-½ for the quarter with the possibility of inequality procedure.

For the C signature with 32nd-note values, I suggest playing eight 32nds to the beat if the texture be made up of continuous or almost continuous 32nds, e.g., the *Prelude in B Flat Major,* WTC I. If the texture is with 32nds occasionally, i.e., the *Prelude in G Minor,* WTC I, and of a heavy or heavily accented character (e.g., with repeated notes in the bass), then I would suggest a Largo or Andante character, i.e., focusing on the 8th note as the beat. In this case the 8th would receive a value of somewhere between T and T-½. The term Andante-Allegro, seen often in the works of D. Scarlatti, signifies an Allegro tempo with even, detached eighth notes.

Tempo Words

Kirnberger clearly states that tempo words affect the speed of the signature. Two of the commonly used terms, Largo and Andante, have a more complex meaning. I believe they both focus on the weaker accent points in the bar. The bow stroke for Largo as described by Quantz is "heavy" and is corroborated by Mozart. Some good examples from Bach would be the *B Minor Fugue,* WTC I (here the accents also occur on the "weak" second and fourth beats); the *G Minor Prelude,* WTC II (here the accents occur on each eighth); the Largo from *Sonata in C Major* for solo violin (here the accents occur on pairs of 16ths). There are many more examples of this type. I would tend to theorize, then, from the music, that Largo accents the "weak" positions of the measure in a "slow" tempo.

Andante is easier to define, as sources generally agree that the term refers to even, separate and equal 8th note motion in the bass, especially, and a "walking" tempo. This would therefore give the appearance of more accents, at least in the bass, and, of course, on the "weak" beats of subdivided beats of the measure.

Here, then, is a chart of how tempo words influence signatures:

Adagissimo . . . . T/2, but slower

Largo . . . . T/2, with increased number of accents

Adagio T/2

Andante . . . . about T-½ + to each 8th, with the 8ths even and separate; also used to contradict inequality of 8th notes

Allegro with C . . . . . . T +

Allegro with ₵ . . . . . . T-½ +

Vivace. . . . . the same as Allegro, but a bit more lively

Presto . . . . T x 2, or thereabouts

Prestissimo. . . . . T x 2 +

The *Concerto in C Major* for two harpsichords, S. 1061, has a second movement which is marked "Adagio ovvero Largo," "Adagio or otherwise Largo." What Bach is telling us is that the tempo can be Adagio with normal accent patterns, that is, 6/8 with 16ths and two accents per bar, *or* it can be Largo, which would mean six accents per bar, using slurred pairs of 16ths. He could hardly mean "slow or otherwise slower"! A further demonstration to show that Largo affects accent as well as tempo is Handel's occasional usage of the term "Largo ma non Adagio."

Example 38: Concerto in C Major for two harpsichords, S. 1061

Quantz adds many words to the ones mentioned above, such as "Allegro assai," "Allegretto," "Adagio cantabile," "Adagio assai" and many subdivisions and qualifications within each category. He states that each of these titles has "a meaning of its own, but refers more to the expression of the dominant passions in each piece than to the tempo proper." (Quantz, p. 284)

Occasionally we see these terms in Bach. This shows that he is using the newer practice of added words qualifying the basic tempo words. Source material does not always give uniform or easily understood definitions of these terms, so we can only be certain of relative values. "Allegro" is somewhat fast, "Vivace" is generally somewhat faster than "Allegro," and "Presto" is faster than "Vivace." It certainly does not seem to be applicable to all pieces marked "Presto." Quantz himself suggests the idea of modification, and says that all references to tempo should be taken with a grain of salt. However, we must be careful about making projections based on our personal preferences when using grains of salt! We at least want to end up in the right ballpark. For a further complication, C.P.E. Bach says that at Berlin "Adagio" is far slower and "Allegro" far faster than is customary elsewhere.

Compound Signatures

When two time signatures are placed next to each other in Bach's music, this indicates that the beat and tempo pattern for the first signature qualify the second signature. This is different from the earlier (ca. 1630) meaning of "compound" signatures, where the denominator referred to the tempo of the preceding section, and the numerator to the new section. In this example, the 12/8 is qualified by the C, slowing the tempo from six 8ths = T, to three 8ths = T, and increasing the number of accented (1 + 3):

Example 39: Jesus Christus unser Heiland, S. 626

Another example of this is the tenor aria from *Cantata No. 7*, "Christ unser Herr zum Jordan kam." The signature is 3/4, 9/8.

Example 40: Cantata No. 7:

Here the beat pattern should follow the rules for 3/4—a strong accent on the first beat, with the second and third beat being weak. The tempo should not, however, be the faster tempo of 3/4, i.e., very fast, but rather the normal 9/8 tempo, or six 8th notes equal to tactus. But Bach evidently did not want the beat pattern for 9/8 in the upper parts, which would dictate a strong accent not only on the first beat, but also a semi-strong accent on the seventh 8th note in each measure as well. Given the beat accent pattern in the continuo (♩. 𝄾 ♪ ♩ ♪), Bach could have written 9/8 instead of 3/4

Another example of this is the *D Major Prelude* from Book II of the *Well Tempered Clavier,* which has a signature of ₵ 12/8.

Example 41: Prelude in D Major, WTC, Book II, S. 874:

The piece is composed with 16th notes as the smallest non-ornamental note value. In 12/8, unqualified by the ₵, there would have to be two strong accents per measure. The ₵ eliminates the second strong accent.

An interesting work to look at that involves more than one time signature is the *E Flat Major Fugue* for Organ, S. 552. Here the signatures are ₵ with quarter notes, 6/4 with 8th notes, and 12/8 with 16ths. One simply keeps the beat throughout: two quarters equals the beat in the first section, six 8ths in the second; and six 16ths in the third.

Bass Activity
... in the First Measure of
Fast-signature Pieces

I will suggest the tempo of "fast" signature (2/4 and most triple meters except for 3/2) compositions should be adjusted, that is, slowed down somewhat, if there is activity in the bass line of the first measure of the composition.

I arrived at this conclusion by looking at the three versions of the opening movement of the *E Major Partita* for violin solo, and by noting differing characteristics (mood, movement, etc.) of pieces written in the same "fast" time signature, e.g., 6/4: *Prelude in C Sharp Minor,* WTC I; and *Fugue in E Flat Major,* 2nd half, S. 552.

The three versions of the partita are for violin, lute and organ with orchestra. The version for violin has no bass activity in the first measure and goes the "full" tempo of 3/4, that is, the fast version of 3/4. This means it goes anywhere from pulse and a half to double pulse. When Bach wrote the version for lute, he knew the lute could not play at as fast a tempo, so he wrote one bass note at the beginning. This slows down the tempo. In the version for organ and orchestra (*Cantata 29,* "Wir danken dir Herr Jesu Christ"), he put two bass notes at the beginning in order to employ an often-used "timpani motiv:"

Example 42: Sinfonia from Cantata 29: Wir danken dir Herr Jesu Christ

As a consequence of this addition, the tempo would have been slowed down too much, so in order to offset that and indicate a faster tempo, he used the qualifying word "Presto;" the faster tempo would be at least violin solo tempo, or perhaps even faster on the organ because of the "Presto."

Example 43: E Major Partita for Violin Solo, S. 1006

Example 44: E Major Suite for Lute, S. 1006a

Example 45: Sinfonia from Cantata 29: Wir danken dir Herr Jesu Christ

If there is no bass activity in the first full measure, it is the full tempo version; if there is bass activity in the first measure, it is a slow, or slower, version for that signature. The more bass activity in the first measure, the slower the tempo.

An example of no bass activity is the *G Major Organ Prelude,* which is in fast 3/4. Since this piece is also qualified by "Vivace," it is probably the fastest piece Bach ever wrote for organ. And if we look at the beginning of the score, we can see that it looks quite empty, utterly uncontrapuntal, as if it were a single violin line accompanied by chords. The reason Bach did not write any organ fugues in 3/4 with 16ths is that they would have been played faster than the organ can easily articulate.

Example 46: Prelude in G Major, S. 541

An example of the relationship between 3/4 and 6/8 is demonstrated by the *A Minor Organ Fugue* and the *Clavier Fugue in A Minor.* The clavier fugue was probably written first, and is in 3/4. The organ fugue was modeled after it, having the same basic theme, but it is written in 6/8. The harmonic pattern is exactly the same, but the organ piece must be played at a more moderate tempo because of the signature. So we see how Bach used 3/4 to indicate a faster tempo, and 6/8 to indicate a more moderate but fast tempo.

Example 47: Clavier Fugue in A Minor, S. 941

Example 48: Fugue in A Minor (Organ), S. 543

This principle is also illustrated in the F Minor Prelude, Book II, WTC. The *Prelude* is in 2/4 with bass activity, the *Fugue* is in 2/4 with no bass activity. We can surmise that the tempo of the *Prelude* is slower than the *Fugue.* (Had Bach wanted the *Prelude* to be played fast, or the usual 2/4 tempo, he would not have put all of the bass notes in the beginning.)

We note that there are no organ fugues with a 2/4 time signature and other fugues written with 2/4 rarely start with the bass voice.

Example 49: Prelude in F Minor, WTC, Book II, S. 881

Example 50: Fugue in F Minor, WTC, Book II, S. 881

Irregular Beat Groupings
... Notes That Do Not Fall into
Regular Divisions of the Beat

It is interesting to see how Bach decides to write out groups of notes that do not fall into the usual metrical groupings of 3, 4, 6, 8 or 12.

In the cadenza from the *Fifth Brandenburg Concerto* he uses this notation for a group of seven notes.

Example 51: Brandenburg Concerto No. 5, S. 1050

But the tempo makes it impossible to perform these seven notes as written. They must be played evenly.

Example 52: Brandenburg Concerto No. 5, S. 1050

It is not possible at that speed to make any of them (other than the first) intrinsically longer or shorter than the others.

The *C Minor Harpsichord Toccata* contains another example of this with a group of nine notes.

Example 53: Toccata in C Minor, S. 911

Again, the tempo dictates that each of the nine notes has the same intrinsic length.

Example 54: Toccata in C Minor, S. 911

It is quite likely that we confuse the written metrical version of an irregular number of notes within a beat with Bach's actual intent, which was that the notes be played with intrinsically equal lengths inside the beat allotted to the group. Another example of this is the *E Major Violin Sonata* with harpsichord obbligato.

Example 55: Sonata No. 3 for Harpsichord and Violin, S. 1016

It is most likely that the notes in this passage should be played in the same amount of time, perhaps with an accelerando.

Example 56: Sonata No. 3 for Harpsichord and Violin, S. 1016

One of the few places where Bach actually wrote an uneven number above a group of notes is in the *Sixth Partita in E Minor* where he writes

Example 57: Partita in E Minor, S. 830

This does not appear to have been one of the conventions of his time, and is quite unusual.

Bravura Works
... Time Signatures and Bravura Pieces

Often when Bach writes a piece in a bravura or brilliant style, he is careful not to introduce fast note values at the beginning of the piece, as that might cause performers to play it at half the speed intended. The bravura passages in both the Fourth and Fifth Brandenburg Concertos occur later in the compositions. The *E Minor Fugue for Organ* (S. 548) also has fast 16th notes that do not appear until after 58 measures of 8th notes.

The *Brandenburg Concerto No. 5* opens with a ₵ time signature with 16ths as the smallest non-ornamental note value.

Example 56: Brandenburg Concerto No. 5, S. 1050

After 46 measures this passage occurs

Example 57: Brandenburg Concerto No. 5, S. 1050

The tempo has already been established at the beginning of the piece as four 16ths equal to a tactus and a half, thus setting the speed for this bravura passage. However, if Bach had used 32nd notes in large quantity at the beginning of the piece, a tempo relying on four 32nd notes as the beat or beat + might have been adopted — certainly much too slow.

Word Accents

Prosody, the study of the art of speech, teaches us what rhythm is, how to place the accents properly, what is long or short. (Mattheson)

Do not keep strict time throughout, but as in the style of the modern madrigals, use here a slow tempo, here a fast one and here one that, as it were, is suspended in the air always in accordance with the expression of the meaning of the words. (Frescobaldi)

These are some interesting descriptions that we have dealing with word accents and meaning. In the preface to *Toccatae* (1617) Frescobaldi advocates using metrical freedoms in the way that madrigalists of his day used them — accenting the words properly, stopping the tempo if necessary in order to make the required accents. This is among the earliest known sources which correlate words with music. Frescobaldi was speaking about the playing of his own keyboard works, and evidently intended them to be played with the same kinds of stress as if they were to be sung. This kind of freedom with the tempo was to be carried over into non-vocal music, and into intabulations (keyboard and lute versions) of vocal music.

If we look at the chorale preludes of Bach, we can find that he used an interesting compositional technique, at least in some of the larger preludes. He took the number of words in a verse, sometimes the number of syllables or the amount of time allotted to syllables, and used this figure to determine the number of measures in the chorale prelude. An interesting example of this is the large version of *Komm Heiliger Geist*. He composed two versions of this, the earlier *Weimar Version,* and a later *Leipzig Version*. The earlier version has 48 measures, which is the number of words in the text, and the later version has 106 measures; the text utilizes 103 half note values and there are three half note rests.

Example 58: Komm, Heiliger Geist, Herre Gott, S. 651

15th Century

Antiphon "Veni Sancte Spiritus", German version in the 16th century by Martin Luther.

56

The concept of stretching the tempo in accordance with the meaning of the words would indicate that measures corresponding to accented syllables could be strong or stretched, and measures corresponding to un-accented syllables would be weak, or passed through more quickly. An interesting example of this is the prelude to *Allein Gott in der Höh sei Ehr.*

Example 59: Allein Gott in der Höh sei Ehr, S. 662a

53 measures

Example 60: Allein Gott in der Höh sei Ehr

53 syllables

"Gloria in excelsis" translated into German by Nikolaus Decius

In compositions where the chorale melody is played clearly without any ornamentation, the stress on the melody would correspond to the word stress instead of a strong or weak measure stress. This is almost certainly what Bach meant when he told his students to play the meaning of the chorale when playing the hymns. He surely did not mean that in performance they should scowl or look agonized when the word "Schmerz" (pain) appeared, but rather that the proper stress of the word patterns or meanings should be brought out in performance by a kind of stretching back and forth in a rubato. Experiment by playing the equivalent strong and weak measures in just that manner; then experiment by playing the strong and weak syllables in that manner as they correspond (notes to text); next experiment by assigning strong and weak characteristics to the measures for musical reasons alone. A similar treatment of chorales occurs occasionally in the *Tablatura Nova* of Scheidt: "Vater unser in Himmelreich" (Canon a 4), and "Da Jesu an dem Kreuze stund." Perhaps Bach derived the idea from Scheidt.

Strong and Weak
... Establishing a Theory for
Strong and Weak Measures

Strong/weak alternations underlie Baroque music at every structural level. As already stated, it is impossible to discuss meters, tempos, accents, fingering, rubato, or almost any other specific performance problem without being aware of the constant presence of alternations between strong and weak, also called "good/bad" or "principal/passing" metric units. This is true whether we are talking about individual notes as subdivisions of the beat, about beats as subdivisions of the measure, or about measures and larger structural units within the piece. The origins of strong-weak occur in chant. Groups of twos and threes (SW, SWW); augmented as tenors of Renaissance music, where their augmented groupings of twos and threes were referred to as "maximodus." This, then, is the origin of strong and weak larger, i.e., measure, subdivisions. Although many sources assume this to be a logical extension of the concept of stressed and unstressed syllables of spoken poetry prominent in the beginnings of Baroque music, ca. 1600, Mattheson went further and said that "in music the possibilities for variation between strong and weak have many levels, compared to poetry which knows only a few." (*Der Vollkommene Kapellmeister,* p. 170, #49) The majority of the German texts of Chorales show simple alternations of strong/weak, strong/weak, and this is indeed a common pattern of alternation found in the music of this period, but we also find, as Mattheson suggested, enormous variations—not only the predictable SWW, or SSW, SWWW or SSWW, but we also find pieces where strong and weak measures follow each other in no particular regular combination.

The following quotation from Quantz gives performers quite specific information about the concept as applied to individual notes, but not measures:

> Here I must make a necessary comment about the length of time each note should be held. One must know how to make a difference in performance between the main notes, also called principal notes, or by the Italians, "good" notes, and the passing notes, also called by some foreigners "bad" notes. Wherever possible, the principal notes must be brought out more strongly than the passing notes. In order to follow this

rule, the fastest notes in every piece in a moderate tempo, or even in an Adagio, even though they appear to have the same value, must be played somewhat unevenly; thus the principal notes of each figure, that is, the first, third, fifth and seventh will be held a little longer than the passing notes, that is, the second, fourth, sixth and eighth; but this holding of the notes should not make as big a difference as the writing of dots beside them would. [Quantz infers gentle—3:2—ratios] When I say "the fastest notes," I mean: quarters in 3/2; eighths in 3/4; sixteenths in 3/8; eighths in Alla breve; sixteenths or thirty-seconds in 2/4 or in common time: but only if there are no groups of notes that are faster, or once again as short, among them, as then these would have to be performed as described above. For example, if one played the eight sixteenth notes in the following examples slowly and equally,

Example 61

they would not sound as pleasing as they would if one played the first and third of each group of four somewhat longer and stronger than the second and fourth.

Other Baroque sources, sometimes in connection with bowing instructions for stringed instruments, discuss the concept of strong and weak measures, not only of strong and weak notes within the measure. Kirnberger gives the best and most complete description of strong and weak measures:

In even meters with 2 beats, and in triple meters, there are melodies in which it is clear that entire measures are alternately heavy and light so that one feels an entire measure to consist of one beat. When the melody is so constructed that one feels the entire measure to be a single beat, then two measures must necessarily be set together to make a single one, with the first part being long, and the second part short.

Later on Turk, in *Klavierschule. . .* 1802, describes a measure's worth with the symbol + . Geminiani says that strong passages must not be accented in a mechanical manner. L. Mozart bows 3/8 measures alternately strong and weak, in his *Violinschule,* 1756, Printz, in *Phrynis Mitileneus,* 1696, says that the first and third measures are inwardly longer than the second and fourth. North, in *North on Music,* 1728, describes measures as "loud" and "soft." The strength or weakness of a measure becomes less important when more than the normal amount of "fastest" note values are placed therein; e.g., a 32nd note texture (i.e., 32 32nds) in common time. This would agree with Kirnberger's set-together measure, made up of measures of smaller duration.

Example 62: St. John Passion, S 245: Tenor Aria No. 32: Erwäge

In this example, the normal accent pattern (in groups of three eighths), is constantly thrown off by the unusual placing of the strong syllables. The normal accent pattern of the measure, on the first and seventh eighth, is further thrown off by accenting of the tenth eighth (first measure of the example), with the beginning of the theme in the bass. Because the piece is in 32nd note values and each measure is large, the "strength" or "weakness" of each measure is of little importance.

Many sources indicate that strong notes or beginning notes of passages should be stretched in time, and, depending on the possibilities of the instrument, should be played louder. It is interesting that when W.A. Mozart and other Classical composers wanted to contradict the normal strong/weak measure progressions, they would often use dynamic markings, usually *f* or *sfz* (historically, an accelerated *messa di voce*. See chapter on violin playing.). The reason they did this was that performers schooled in the Baroque and early Classical tradition considered measures in terms of strong/weak unless marked otherwise.

Example 63: Mozart: Sonata, K. 270:

The example is curious in two ways: (a) it is a six measure grouping; and (b) one measure (m. 2) is duplicated as measure 4 with a sudden change of dynamic. In this example the normal strong/weak progressions would have been SWSWWS. The sudden *f* in measure 4 makes that measure strong (SWWSWS) in contrast with its counterpart in measure 2.

Before the 1750's, many sources discussing performance speak specifically about rhythmic alternations, suggesting changes in duration rather than changes in dynamics. Forkel, writing in 1802 of Bach's playing, said that he usually played rather briskly, but managed to introduce so much variety that each piece became a conversation. J.G. Walther's dictionary article, entitled *"Quantitas Notarum extrinsica & intrinsica"* discusses the difference between the extrinsic and intrinsic time values of notes, that is, the difference between the way they appear on a page, and the way they sound in performance.

It is evident that one performer alone will have greater options and obligations in the use of these rhythmic alternations than will a group of performers. So it is, above all, music written for the keyboard or for an unaccompanied string instrument that presents the performer with the problem of finding and distinguishing between the strong and weak structural elements. Performers in music using more than one or two players must, of course, be just as aware of the strong/weak alternations, but the rhythmic deviations will be smaller and fewer. Historically, then, strong and weak measure theory or description starts at the end of the 17th century and terminates about 1850 with Liszt's objection to downbeat accentuation. As stated before, F. Liszt referred in a letter of 1856 to a

> mode of playing, still customary in some places . . . a mechanical kind of playing which, *meticulously adhering to the metre, splits up the performance by perpetually emphasizing the strong and weak beats.*

He stated that he did not wish this kind of rhythmic convention to be applied to his compositions, but preferred

> only that kind of periodic style of execution which emphasizes the essential accents and displays the nuances of the music by means of melodic and rhythmic shaping.

Even melodic lines of the Brahms-Wagner era are written with strong-weak measure considerations.

Example 64: J. Brahms: Symphony No. 4 in E Minor, Op. 98, 1st Mvt.

During the Baroque and early Classical period, there was an important strong-weak measure consciousness. Later music echoed this consideration but in a more unconscious manner. We have already seen how to determine the strong and weak beats within the measure. How do we determine which measures are strong? In general, a measure is strong

1) If the theme begins on a downbeat:

Example 65: Toccata in D (Dorian), S. 538

2) If there is a cadence in any part of the measure. (However, short measures, two by two, will often have the cadence "weak.")

3) If there is a chord on the downbeat of a measure in a thin texture, the chord sometimes takes more time than the measure allows:

Example 66: Italian Concerto, S. 971

4) If the texture of a measure is thicker than that of the measures preceding it:

Example 67: Prelude in G Major, S. 541

5) If the downbeat has an ornament:

Example 68: Fantasia in G Minor, S. 542

6) If there is a large leap after the note on the downbeat or third beat:

Example 69: Suite in F Major, Prelude, S. 809

Example 70: Italian Concerto, S. 971

7) Dissonance will tend to be strong:

Example 71: Partita #3 for Violin Solo, S. 1006

Regarding weak measures,
   1) If there is a tie from the previous measure onto or over the down-beat, the measure is generally weak:

Example 72: English Suite No. 5, Prelude, S. 810

   2) If there is a series of sequences, for instance, a statement and three repetitions, the statement is strong, the first repetition is weak, the second repetition is strong, and the last repetition is weak. A statement with two repetitions would normally be SWW.

Example 73: Fugue in C Major, S. 870

Example 74: Toccata in D Minor, S. 538

This example deviates from the normal accent pattern. Holding slightly the 3rd count of the 2nd measure would then indicate the change of direction in the sequential pattern.

Sometimes we can theorize a measure to be *somewhat* strong or weak because of its context. The analysis of the Italian Concerto will illustrate this. Sometimes measures are ambiguous. It is still better to assign them some S or W significance, since in the Baroque and early Classical style each measure has its own degree of S or W. Türk in *Klavierschule. . . ,* brings the concept of somewhat strong into prominence with his markings + + + = S, + + = somewhat S, and + = W. This theory is clearer if we remember the influence of word accents, the importance of poetry and the spoken word as a model for music during the Baroque era. (See p. 58) For instance, much of Shakespeare falls into iambic pentameter, that is, five metrical feet, each consisting of a weak syllable and a strong syllable. Many people will remember tedious hours in school spent analyzing this scansion and noting exceptions, usually to the detriment of any appreciation of the beauty or importance of the language and its content.

But if we look at just a few familiar lines, we can readily see how relative the terms "strong" and "weak" must be.

1. Oh that this too too so- lid flesh would melt

or

2. But soft what light through yon- der win- dow breaks
   it is the east and Ju- liet is the sun.

however

3. Friends, Ro- mans count- ry men lend me your ears

Each foot consists of W-S, but it is clear that not all strong syllables are equally strong. It is clear, too, that some feet, and even some lines, are stronger than others. Anyone who reads these lines *must* break away from a rigorous observance of metrical exactitude. The options in finding the relative strength and weakness (both in duration and dynamics) of not only each syllable (read "note") but also each foot (read "measure") are what will make the difference between a monotonous, mechanical series of words, and a vehicle for meaning.

Example 75: Fugue in F Sharp Major, WTC II, S. 882

This complex example is a series of repetitions of the formula 𝅘𝅥 𝅘𝅥 | 𝅗𝅥 𝅗𝅥 and 𝄽 𝅘𝅥 | 𝅘𝅥 𝅘𝅥 . The S or W is assigned to statement or repetition respectively.

The following example from the *Toccata in F Major, S. 540* is exceptional:

Example 76: Toccata in F Major, S. 540

This shows the statement followed by five repetitions, all of them weak because of their 7-6 descending series. A repetition series, ascending by step motion, will often have a "strong" effect.

3) If the first measure material begins on a rest, that measure is weak:

Example 77: Fugue in C Major, WTC I, S. 846

Although it is usual to have strong and weak measures in patterns or alternation, we also find very irregular patterns. The *E Minor Organ Prelude* ("The Wedge") is an interesting example. The descending runs in the left hand have strong measures where the hand must stop at the bottom to leap back to the beginning of the next scale down. The alternate measures are weak. This is normal.

Example 78: Prelude in E Minor (The Wedge), S. 548

Then at the end of the prelude we have an extraordinary example of five strong measures in a row. One is forced to pause at the beginning of each of these measures to make the leap. This pause for the leap automatically lengthens the measure slightly, making it strong.

Example 79: Prelude in E Minor, (The Wedge), S. 548

Similar strings of "strong measures" occur in poetry, usually as a series of exclamatory statements with a pause or dynamic accent on each one.

From *Macbeth,* Act IV, Scene III, MacDuff is being told (in iambic pentameter) of the murder of his family.

(MacDuff)   My Children too?

(Ross)   Wife, children, servants all

that could be found . . .

The normal scansion is marked above, but it is obvious that a "performance" of these lines forces the word "wife" to be strong, making a series of three strong syllables in a row.

To create an even more dramatic effect, Shakespeare forces a whole series of strong syllables by breaking out of iambic pentameter. An example of this is in *Julius Caesar,* Act III, Scene II; the citizens of Rome break into Antony's speech over the dead body of Caesar.

. . . Revenge! About! Seek! Burn!

Fire! Kill! Slay! Let not a traitor live. . .

The concept of strong and weak beats and measures points out interesting differences to the beat pattern in the progressive statements of the fugue subject in the *G Minor Organ Fugue.* The fugue subject enters at different metrical points, sometimes starting in a weak measure, sometimes in a strong measure. The fugue opens on a weak position in the first measure. Hence this measure is called "weak" within our theory. The subject does not start on a downbeat. When the subject enters in the pedal, it is stressed by entering on the downbeat of a strong measure. This means that it has to be accented differently. The accent pattern of the musical material when it is first introduced is:

Example 80: Fugue in G Minor, S. 542

Interestingly enough, measure 4 would be called S since the downbeat is at the end of the cadential drive of the subject.

When it is introduced in the pedal it is:

Example 81: Fugue in G Minor, S. 542

The next step is to put the strong/weak patterns into larger groups to determine if the larger pattern is in duple (strong/weak, strong/weak), triple (S/W. S/W, S/W), or an irregular category.

There are various ways to differentiate or highlight a strong measure. The most important one is to prolong the downbeat (or other important beat) somewhat. The actual duration of the held note will, of course, vary with the situation. Experiment with holding it for approximately the value of an additional 32nd note, presuming a context of 16th notes. The time that is added to make this accent is not subtracted elsewhere in the measure. The approach to the held beat or note should be "rounded," i.e., very, very slightly retarded.

If one were to relegate numerically, in common time, the following "strengths" or amounts of accent holds on a scale of one to three, the downbeat of a strong measure would be worth 3; the third count of the strong measure would be 2; the downbeat of the weak measure would be worth 2; the third count of the weak measure would be 1. These numbers are, of course, totally arbitrary, They give, however, an idea of the duration of accents we can employ. Even when there are several weak measures in a row, the accent pattern remains the same. The downbeat of the weak measure is slight and the third count is almost imperceptible. The "one" (1) used for the latter is very weak, almost imperceptible, and sometimes not perceptible by the ear but only by the mind.

It is often a good idea to add an ornament on some part of the downbeat chord so that the time needed for prolongation can be taken without the awkwardness which might be produced if one were simply to hold the chord. Interestingly enough, Mattheson refers to bad (weak) chords as those devoid of the slightest ornamentation! (*Grosse General-Bass Schule,* p. 364)

If the downbeat accent in a strong measure has been displaced to some other beat, then the displaced accent receives the impetus of the strong measure and is treated just as if it were the actual downbeat of the measure. In general, then, the patterns one finds in Bach are (a) S W, (b) S W W, S (S) W, 4/4 subdivided / / / | / / / / | / / / / | / / / / or
hemiola at triple meter cadences.   1   2   3   1   2   3   1

Example 70: Italian Concerto, S. 971

The Strongs are contrary to the equivalent passage at the beginning because of the different bass texture.

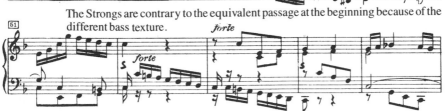

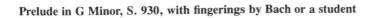

Prelude in G Minor, S. 930, with fingerings by Bach or a student

Irregular Beat Alterations

There are further examples of alterations in the normal beat patterns. Some of these occur when the passage is divided in a certain way between the two hands. At a fast tempo this causes the normal beat pattern to be broken. Some examples of this are:

    1) The *D Minor Harpsichord Concerto,* S. 1052, one hand

Example 82: D Minor Harpsichord Concerto, S. 1052

    2) The *Chromatic Fantasy and Fugue,* S. 903, two hands

Example 83: Chromatic Fantasy and Fugue, S. 903

    3) The *B Flat Major Prelude* from the First Book, S. 866

Example 84: Prelude in B Flat Major, S. 866

4) The *D Major Fugue* for Organ, S. 532

Example 85: Fugue in D Major, S. 532

The counter-subject clarifies matters later.
  5) Gigue from the "English" *Suite in G Minor,* S. 808

Example 86: Gigue from the "English" Suite in G Minor, S. 808

  6) The *Toccata in D Major,* Allegro, S. 912

Example 87: Toccata in D Major, Allegro, S. 912

In this example Bach shifts the main accent to the third beat, the three quarter notes before act as if they were 𝄽 ♩♩♩ | ♩ .

  A change in the beat pattern is also caused if the composer writes deliberately against the beat pattern, either shifting the downbeat to 2, 3, or 4 (3 is the most usual in common time; See "set-together" measures, p. 29),

Example 88: Fugue in C Major, WTC Book I, S. 846

or hemiola, or substitutes a different beat pattern from the one the signature would normally dictate, e.g., 3/4 or 3/2 on 4/4.

Example 89: Fugue in D Minor (Dorian), S. 538

Often this change is indicated by the addition of chords. The example from the *Allemanda* of the *B Minor Violin Partita* is exceptional.

Example 90: B Minor Violin Partita: Allemanda, S. 1002

In this example, Bach places the triple and quadruple stopping at irregular points, completely throwing off the normal accent patterns. The third measure is clearly strong as it is a cadence measure. However Bach chooses not to emphasize it in any way, although it is linearly the end of a "third" motion.

Example 91:

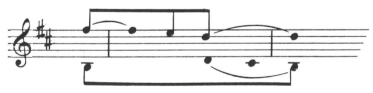

From the *B Minor Mass:* "Laudamus te," the beat shift in measure six is very unusual.

Rubato

The word "rubato" is used fairly loosely to describe any of a variety of rhythmic alterations which should be considered separately. For our purposes, we will define three kinds of rubato:

1) The time "robbed" in one place is given back in another. One example of this would be the slight lengthening of the first note of a slurred, four-note group compensated by the relative shortening of the other three notes.

2) Time is "robbed" (agogic accent, or rhythmic freedom) with no compensation made. The different possibilities for this in connection with the structural concepts of strong and weak beats, and strong and weak measures, are discussed in detail (see p. 58) This is the most controversial kind of rubato and the one that often bothers listeners who are unaccustomed to it. If, for example, the piece begins on a strong measure and the first beat is only a single chord, there is no way to make clear the strength of the measure other than by taking time and not giving it back. It is possible to emphasize strong beats with the rubato described in (1), but only in measures where there is enough note motion that notes in the latter part of the measure may be compressed to compensate for the stretched notes. The second kind of rubato, in which time taken is not given back, is historically an important one. Quantz and Mozart say the value of the measure, however, should not be altered. Although this may appear to be contradictory to this second type of rubato, this is really not the case. I do not believe they were thinking in terms of precise scientific measurement, but rather were suggesting that the rhythmic "feel" of the measure should not be altered.

Quantz's and Mozart's statements were, I believe, important admonitions that the performer should never allow the latitude of rhythmic alteration to alter the predictable feeling of the basic beat. These statements have a reformatory quality about them, as if license was being taken that they considered unacceptable and disorienting.

3) The third example applies to accompanied works for solo voice or solo instrument. The bass line carries a steady beat and the solo line is free to fall behind or go ahead of the bass line. Tosi, an Italian authority on vocal performance, writing in 1732, said that the expression "tempo rubato" (stolen time) particularly speaks to vocal performance or performance on a single instrument in the Pathetic and Tender mode. The

bass has an exactly regular pace, the other part retards or anticipates in a singular manner, for the sake of expression (p. 219-220). Tosi's work, *Opinioni de Cantori antichi e moderni,* was translated into German by Agricola (J.F. Agricola, *Anleitung zur Singkunst,* 1757, a student of J.S. Bach), who noted these possibilities for this kind of rubato. This third type is described by Türk in the same manner (*Klavierschule. . . ,)*

Example 93

The amount of time taken depends on whether the rubato points fall on a strong or weak beat, within a strong or weak measure.

Tosi also mentions "stealing the time and returning the theft," and other kinds of expressive rubato: ". . . 'Risvegliato,' ('awakened'), after having sung languishingly or dreamily, one should suddenly revive the measure . . . making it more lively and gay. . . ; 'Stretto Serre,' 'pressed together,' . . . very fast . . . 'Tempo Regiato' . . . pausing on expressive notes."

The apparent rushing and holding back that we hear in a stylistically correct performance of music of this period is the result of these different kinds of rubatos functioning together.

It is evident that the principles governing these rhythmic alterations and freedoms are not exempt from gross exaggeration and misapplication. On the other hand, they must not be ignored or denied as they were during the period in which such phrases as "utmost precision," and "mathematical exactitude" were used to describe Bach's music. It is only when these principles are applied that a work of this period can, in fact, achieve an artistic unity and focus.

Fringing

Another device for emphasis is called "fringing." This term was first used by Roger North and recovered recently by Sol Babitz. Fringing is used to emphasize strong metrical units. Passages written to be played simultaneously are unsynchronized for emphasis, i.e., the notes of one hand are played slightly before or after the notes of the other hand, even if they appear to be written together. North described it as the mixing of the note with the one before or behind it "which doth not corrupt but rather fringes the tone..." He also said that when two notes are played "to a tough together," nothing is achieved by the doubling except "a little loudness, but in the other way by frequent dissonances there is a pleasant seasoning obtained." (*North on Music,* p. 172)

There are two ways of achieving this effect. In the first instance, the bass is played slightly before the upper voice, i.e., the soprano can be played slightly late or the bass played slightly early. The delayed soprano is indicated and referred to by Couperin and by other French writers as "suspension." (This has nothing to do with contrapuntal suspension.) When the bass note is played slightly before the upper voices (whether it was played on the beat or slightly before the beat), the effect is often that the bass sounds slightly before the beat. The later French Baroque performers Duphly and Forqueray also deal with this phenomenon. The following examples show how and when this kind of fringing can be used:

Example 94: Prelude in C Minor, WTC, Book I, S. 847

The second way to create this effect is to take the last note of a beat and add it to the first note of the next beat. The following example from the *E Flat Major Prelude* for Organ, S. 552, illustrates this:

Example 95: Prelude in E Flat Major, S. 552

The works of J.S. Bach are full of places where the latter type of fringing is used. Together with arpeggiation and the addition of a chord or ornament, fringing is a very helpful device for performance accent on the harpsichord. Because the sound of the harpsichord dies away relatively quickly, simply stopping on the strong beat(s) of the strong measure can make a rather abrupt or awkward effect. Here it is unfortunately not the sound of the note which is lengthened, but the gap between the strong note or beat and the next note or beat. The effect of a held note is obviously quite different on the organ, violin and voice.

Fringing can be used on the organ only in passages for the manuals. It is not advisable to fringe while using the pedals, as this usually produces an awkward stumbling effect. A classical organ, which has a built-in acoustic, is so rich from a harmonic standpoint that the bass on the manuals can be played slightly before the upper notes without creating this awkward effect. In the words of North, one is "not corrupting, but rather fringing the tone." Here is an example from Couperin of "suspension" or "fringing:"

Example 96: Couperin: Les Plaisirs de St. Germaine

Inequality and Pairs of Notes

Inequality is the term used to describe the practice of playing notes in an uneven or unequal fashion, even though the notes appear to be intrinsically equal in length:

Example 97

The two most common ways of varying equally written notes are by using a long-short (LS) pattern or else a short-long (SL) pattern. Regarding the SL or LS patterns, there are several ways of performing these in terms of the ratio between the short and the long. The more commonly used ratios are 2:3 or 3:2, and 1:3 or 3:1. In order to translate these ratios into note values, add the two numbers of the ratio together; if the ratio is 2:3, the total is five and then the first note is worth 2/5s and the second note worth 3/5s of the count. In the ratio of 3:1 the first note is worth 3/4s and the second note worth 1/4 of the count, as if notated with conventional dots. Ratios with a total of five produce a gentle, rocking effect. Ratios with a total of four are more angular and give a stronger feeling of unevenness.

Example 98: Loulié, Eléments de la Musique (Supplement)

Although, according to Dom Gregory Murray and Wollaert, the subject of ratios and inequality goes back to Gregorian chant, one of the first important historical sources to mention inequality is Frescobaldi. He discusses it in connection with a performance of a series of pairs of notes. Sancta Maria, at the end of the Renaissance and the beginning of the

Baroque period, suggests that eighths can be played SL, LS, or SSSL. When one plays the music of Cabezón and the Spanish music of that period in this altered manner, artfully choosing one of the options, the music becomes a revelation rather than mere tedium (as frequently heard). Caccini (*Nuove Musiche,* 1601), also, discusses alterations of pairs of notes. Inequality, except for the unusual type mentioned by Sancta Maria (SSSL), sometimes used in the 17th and 18th century "overture style," is concerned with alteration of pairs of notes, slurred or unslurred. Inequality is a hallmark of the French Baroque, described in treatises from the late 1600s through most of the 18th century.

Inequality is a product of keyboard technique when slurs arc added to a series of paired notes at a fast tempo (ca. 108). Inequality is also grounded in physiological or technical reasons. This can be demonstrated by first playing the following passage at a moderate tempo, not slurring, and keeping the notes equal:

Example 99

Now add slurs 4 2 4 2 4 2 and gradually increase the tempo. As you accelerate the tempo, observe the slur pattern; the movement from the first note into the second is legato, but the movement from the second into the first of the next pair is not. You will observe that an inequality pattern becomes inevitable as the speed gradually increases. The first note of each pair becomes shorter, and the second proportionately longer. It is the addition of the slur at a fast tempo that opened the way to inequality in keyboard music. Technically, it is the combination of slurred pairs with the same fingerings on each pair, in a brisk tempo that gives us SL inequality. Whenever we see slurred pairs in fast keyboard music of any era, from Frescobaldi to Schönberg, they will be played as SL. An example of this is the final movement of Beethoven's *Opus 78,* which must be played in SL pairs.

Example 100: Beethoven: Sonata for Piano, Op. 78

Fingering and Rhythmic Modification

We read of Bach's own playing, that his fingering resembled a hen scratch. His fingertips must have pulled in and up. This probably refers primarily to clavichord technique, but would certainly have been used on the harpsichord and organ as well. It was common keyboard technique of the time to "throw" a finger over another finger, usually three over four or two over three, and to pull the first finger out of the way. This is in contrast to the more modern way of playing passages by passing the thumb under the fingers. For instance, in a scale passage fingered as follows:

Example 101

one would retract the fourth finger, which resembled "scratching" and was the basis of harpsichord technique in the old style. The fingering patterns that we have from that time, show us that it was considered proper to keep the hand as closed into one position as possible. Here is a "Baroque" fingering and a modern fingering for a passage from the double harpsichord *Concerto in C Minor,* S. 1062:

Example 102: Concerto in C Minor for Two Harpsichords, S. 1062

I think it is possible to make a real case for the Baroque fingering. The hand is simply pulled out of its first position and immediately moved into the second position. This is done by "scratching away" the third finger, producing a musically sensitive articulation, plus a shortening of the "scratching." As the finger retracts, the hand moves to another position. This is very much in contrast to the modern style of piano technique in which hand positions move from close to open and back again, with the fingers constantly spreading apart and being drawn together.

Quantz said about Bach's playing, "[he is] one of the greatest of all clavier players," "... in the execution of running notes, one should not lift the fingers as soon as they have played, but should pull the tips of them over the keys letting them glide [this would refer to retracting] off the keys." *(Versuch einer Anweisung die Flöte traversière zu spielen, p. 232)*

On the front page of *Parthenia* (1611) there is a picture of a girl playing a keyboard instrument. Her hand position looks unusual to us, and it has even been suggested that she was, in fact, deformed; but she is simply using her hands in this "scratching out" style. She has just retracted her fourth finger and the third is already playing, or possibly she is about to retract her third finger and play with the second finger. The position of her hand is quite in contrast to modern playing but is necessary to the crossing of three over four. This technique was used not only for the harpsichord, but also for the clavichord and the organ.

On another front page, this time *Musicks Hand-maide,* by Playford, we see again a demonstration of the three over four principle. The young lady's left-hand fifth finger is off the keyboard. Her fourth finger is retracted as if her third finger were about to go over it. It may seem somewhat foolish to place credence in what these plates tell us, but they do show the basic hand position and a few of the finger positions characteristic of the time.

Muſicks Hand-maide
Preſenting New and Pleaſant LESSONS
FOR THE
Virginals or Harpſycon.

Gui: Faue: an Saup:

London,Printed for *John Playford* at his Shop in the *Temple.* 1663.

The older combinations of finger patterns were usually limited to seven or eight notes played in one direction with one hand. One would normally encounter one or two "scratch-overs" (r.h. 1,2,3,4,3,4,3,4) in such a passage. One does not ordinarily find longer passages of scale-writing in one direction in older music, except in virtuosic music. When a longer passage of fast notes occurs in Bach, his own manuscripts show that the stemming of the notes and the beams often changes to indicate that the passage is broken up between the two hands.

Example 103: Partita in G Major, S. 829

Passing the thumb under is, of course, a basic element of keyboard technique today. This was not the case in Bach's time. The keys of the instruments were narrower and much shorter front to back. It would have been difficult to use this technique, as it would produce an undesirable accent or heaviness on the note played by the thumb. Even though thumb-passing was not common, Bach undoubtedly used it, as can be seen from this passage.

Example 104: Italian Concerto, Third Mvt., S. 971

This passage would be almost impossible to execute at a fast tempo without passing the thumb. Although Bach probably used this technique himself, he likely did not teach it to beginning students. The thumb was used occasionally on sharp or flat notes, the player's concern being to keep the hand in one position while avoiding the use of the thumb on these notes. Bach had a "rule of thumb" for fingering, quoted by Kirnberger, who said that in most cases the thumb falls on the note before or after the tonic, i.e., the leading tone and the supertonic.

In Baroque music, fingering patterns very often correspond to note patterns. There are many examples from Diruta, Sancta Maria and Bull

(English Virginal school). The following example is by Diruta; the "strong fingers" are two and four:

Example 105: Diruta: Il Transilvan, Venice 1625

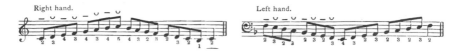

In the next example by Bull, the strong fingers here are three and occasionally one.

Example 106: John Bull: Preludium (before 1599) (GE II, p. 34)

The essential feature of all the early schools of keyboard fingering is the use of "good" (i.e., strong) fingers on "good" (accented) notes, and of "bad" (weaker) fingers on unaccented notes. The Italian and early German fingering (ca. 1600) was based on the designation of the second and fourth digits as the good fingers (hence, perhaps, the myth that "the thumb was never or rarely used in early fingerings" because of its unstressed position in the system). Opposed to this was the fingering based on fingers one, three and five as the "good" digits. This offered more versatility, and is the basis of the fingering of the virginalists and of the 17th and 18th century French and Germans.

In 1717 Couperin gave us the fingerings for consecutive thirds in one hand. One can study his more complex fingering patterns in his *L'art de toucher le clavecin.*

Example 107: Couperin: L'art de toucher le clavecin

The Praetorius quote shows us how truly flexible early fingering was:

> Many think it a matter of great importance and despise such organists as do not use this or that particular fingering, which in my opinion is not worth the talk: for let a player run up and down with either first, middle, or third finger, aye even with his nose if that could help him, provided everything is done clearly, correctly, and gracefully, it does not much matter how or in what manner it is accomplished.
>
> Michael Praetorius: *De Organographia Syntagma Musicum,* II,
> Wolfenbüttel, 1619

We will now examine some examples from Bach. These fingerings are almost unavoidable.

Example 108: Chromatic Fugue, S. 903

The *Concerto in A Major* for Harpsichord contains a good passage to practice for the "feel" of Baroque fingerings. The changing finger must be snapped:

Example 109: Concerto in A Major for Harpsichord, S. 1055

The fingerings are by a student of Bach's: J.C. Vogler. One can experiment with the kinds of rhythmic modifications they suggest.

Example 109a: Fugue in C Major, S. 870

Table of Fingering and Slur Stylizations

1. 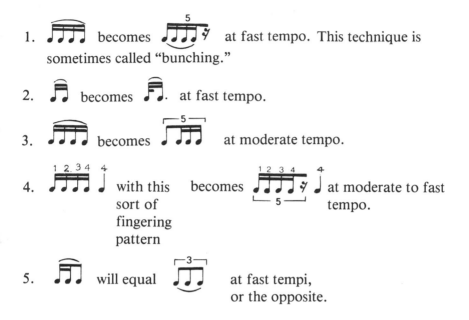 becomes at fast tempo. This technique is sometimes called "bunching."

2. becomes at fast tempo.

3. becomes at moderate tempo.

4. with this sort of fingering pattern becomes at moderate to fast tempo.

5. will equal at fast tempi, or the opposite.

Five-Digit Patterns

Example 110: Scarlatti, Sonata in G, K. 14

Example 111: Bach: Partita in B Minor, S. 831

Although we do not have written in fingerings, the 1,2,3,4,5 fingerings are certainly correct.

This passage, from the *C Sharp Major Fugue,* WTC I would probably have been played with the given fingering. We can infer this from the shortness of the keys and the difficulty of passing the thumb. This fingering also gives a natural time accent to the first note of each group, as well as a slight clipping of the last note of each group. All of this is stylistically desirable.

Example 112: Fugue in C Sharp Major, WTC I, S. 848

Stylizations from the Literature

Forced note value alterations:

Example 113: Concerto in C Major for Two Harpsichords, S. 1061

Forced time on the downbeat:

Example 114: Concerto in C Minor for Two Harpsichords, S. 1060

The slurs will sound .

This fingering is not unavoidable but quite likely.

Example 115: Concerto in C Minor for Two Harpsichords, S. 1060

The  will sound like . This is especially true at faster tempi.

Example 116: Trio Sonata No. 2 in C Minor

Here is an interesting example of a pre-Bachian "forced" rubato:

Example 117: Sweelinck: Fantasia Chromatica, m. 56

In this example, the tactus would occur on the first of four eighths. The 32nds would be almost impossible to execute at that tempo, forcing a rubato.

Post-Bachian "forced" rubato:

Example 118: Beethoven: Op. 31

In this example, the third beat of the measure can in no way be played in time. (Czerny gives 144 to the quarter.)

From both these examples and countless written out trills at the ends of measures (especially in Elizabethan music), one can discern a tendency to slow down the beat (beats) before a cadential occurrence.

Inequality and Note Holding

The kinds of inequality produced in keyboard music have to do with the nature of the organ or harpsichord, as distinct from the modern piano. On organs and harpsichords, the dynamic level of the notes is predetermined. Once the registration is set, the performer has no control over dynamic intensity. The opposite is true of the piano (hence the name of the instrument, the pianoforte). When one plays at or in excess of M.M. 126 (approximately) on the piano, the tendency is for the notes to become dynamically unequal rather than rhythmically unequal. If you play the simple passage of unslurred pairs shown on page 90 or any continuous succession of notes, you will see that when the speed becomes so great that literal mechanical evenness is no longer possible, the first element to become uneven on the piano is the dynamic level. Some notes become noticeably louder or softer than others. On the harpsichord or the organ, fast playing produces rhythmic unevenness of adjacent notes rather than dynamic inequality. This unevenness is independent of the technical proficiency of the performer.

It seems reasonable that both the physical possibilities and the physical limitations of any instrument are primary influences on the development of the style of music for the instrument. These effects, then, become stylized and are carried over into music for other instruments, regardless of whether the original limitations still hold true. One example of this is the stylization of slurred pairs into "Scotch snaps" (also called "Lombard rhythm" or "coulé"), which, as explained, is unavoidable on the harpsichord and organ at a fast tempo. An increase in tempo will cause a similar tendency in string instruments. Although it is technically easier because of bowing technique to get around the difficulty and maintain the equality, the tendency remains. It is quite likely that inequality in slurred or unslurred pairs, and the holding of first notes of slur groupings, also occurs in early string writing. In Samuel Scheidt's *Tabulatura Nova* (1624), we see slurs of groups of two and four notes. When he marks these slurs, he often writes "imitatio violistica" ("imitation of viol-bowing style"). The slurred effect created by the playing of a group of notes in one bow most certainly was imitated by keyboard instruments and became stylized in all music, regardless of the instrument or its particular possibilities or limitations.

Example 119: Samuel Scheidt: Tablatura Nova

In slower music, slurred pairs also came to be played in this kind of inequality. This was a stylized result of the necessities of the faster tempi. In slow tempi, where the inequality stylization is introduced, one is not limited to short/long, but can use long/short as well. Long/short is, in fact, the norm in moderate tempo music. This is characteristic of French Baroque music, not to be confused with the inequality "effect" resulting from the held first note of a slurred pair in fast tempi.

Inequality was practiced differently in Italy than in France, and was more common in France. Its use was not unified during its great period. In France the eighth was generally subject to inequality; in Italy the sixteenth was the note value used for inequality. (For a tabulation of French inequality procedure see p. 322, The French Inégales ... JAMS, No. 3, 1965. In this chart Frederick Neumann has catalogued exhaustively the important French sources on inequality.) In an early Italian example from Caccini, most of the descending pairs are short/long and the ascending pairs are LS (*Nouve Musiche,* 1601). Monteclair (1709) said, "all descending pairs are best played as SL."

Example 120

All national styles during the Baroque use inequality to some degree; differing ratios and restrictions determine the relationships of the short and long. Extreme dotting is usually associated with Italy. The most common ratio was probably 3:2, called "lourer" in France. Three-to-one ratio and the more extreme ratios are also found in French music. This style is called "pointer" or "piqué." French music was written with the inequality procedures clearly in mind. One of the first instances of written out inequality occurs in the introduction of G. Corrette's *Livre d'Orgue* (1703). According to Muffat and others, eighths in cut time were played unequally in the French style but not in the Italian style. This is probably why Couperin says, "We dot our eighth notes where foreigners do not." He is actually talking about specific "note" value inequality when saying, "We play their music better than they play ours."

The fact that different ratios of inequality, as well as articulation silences existed is demonstrated by the music boxes and cylinders of Baroque times. In the writings of Dom Bedos and others, we find precise directions for the insertion of pins into cylinders in order to get the desired ratios and the silences of articulation.

Example 121: Dom Bedos

Specific instances of inequality are also found in English music, e.g., two versions of the *Purcell Suite in G,* one with the inequality written in, and one omitting it.

Example 122: Purcell: Suite in G: Allmand (from Oxford, Christ Church MS 1177)

Probably the 8th note was the value most commonly used for inequality during the French Baroque. This was especially true of the "organ mass" style. In the later French Baroque, 16th notes were also commonly used for inequality. In French style in general, the note level used for inequality varied, e.g., 8ths in 3/2 or 2 or $\frac{2}{2}$; 16ths or eighths in C, 2/4.

It is evident that inequality involves a consideration of the strong/weak concept that underlies almost every aspect of performance of music of this era. Bedos, for instance, gives directions for unequal performance of series of 8th notes, but prescribes different ratios depending on the place of the note grouping within the measure. Couperin and Bedos specifically state that dissonant pairs on a "good" beat should be played as SL.

Matteis, an important violinist of the Baroque, suggests holding the first note of a slurred grouping. Quantz suggests holding the first note of 3, 4, 6, or 8 note groupings. L. Mozart says to hold the first note of a slur, but not if it falls on a rhythmically weak note. It appears that, in any case, the lengthening of notes under strong-beat slurs would be more than under weak-beat slurs. Slur patterns are also stylized in many ways, depending on the tempo of the passage. (see p. 99)

It should be added here that there are various factors other than nationalistic ones which influence the type of inequality one chooses. Various ratios may be employed depending on the acoustics, the instrument, or the occasion!

Quantz and the major French sources generally agree on those conditions that would preclude inequality. Passages should be played evenly, with no inequality, under the following conditions: If there are repeated notes, if there are large skips, if the tempo is fast, if there is a texture with triplets, with slurring over more than two notes, or if qualified with words understood by the conventions of the time to preclude inequality, e.g., Croches égales, Martéle, Mesuré, etc. Dots or dashes over notes were another notational symbol to indicate that the notes should be played in even rhythms. Allemandes were also generally not subject to inequality.

There are restrictions for French inequality and one might draw the conclusion that it was used somewhat less than most performers and scholars suggest today. Composers sometimes wrote only a few measures of a piece in inequality or dotted notes, and then to spare themselves and the copyists a good deal of unnecessary labor, they would write the rest of the piece with equal notes. It seems likely that it was understood by the performers of their day that the entire piece should be played in the inequality pattern indicated at the beginning of the piece. A famous instance of this occurs in Bach in the tenor-soprano duet, Domine Deus, from the *B Minor Mass*. Bach wrote the first few measures of the flute solo, in the flute part only, indicating the desired dotting or inequality.

Example 123: B Minor Mass, S. 232, No. 7

Flauto traverso

Throughout the rest of the piece, the analogous passages are written evenly for both the flute and the voices, albeit with slurs added. The snapped rhythms are certainly continued. The second violin and viola are dotted in the parts of a Bach autograph score.

Another example would be the Händel Fugue in D Minor from the *Suite in D Minor:*

Example 124: Handel: Suite in D Minor: Fugue

Here one plays the entire fugue in dotted rhythms.

Another example of this is found in the "Trauerode, Cantata 198." It is difficult to imagine how this could be performed, if the voices were not intended to match the instruments' dotting.

Example 125: Cantata No. 198: Trauerode

Inequality, though quite independent of metric accent, has its birth in the strong and weak ideals of this period. The LS patterns of inequality are, of course, strong and weak in their implication. Inequality procedure is less selective than metric accent, since it is used throughout the texture of a composition suited for inequality treatment.

It is the author's conclusion that inequality in France was employed, for the most part, in 2:1 ratios (triplets); that 3:2 ratios were used by skilled players for instances where a more gentle quality (to the pairs) would have been artistically desirable. (Perhaps one reason for a performance of two eights as triplets was the non-uniform usage of the "3" bracket to indicate a triplet); that 3:1 ratios were generally written as dotted eighth followed by sixteenth, rather than performed that way from two equally written eights;

Example 126: Couperin: Le Gaillard-Boiteux

that the figure: dotted eighth-sixteenth was often underdotted (e.g., Le Gaillard-Boiteux, 18th Ordre, F. Couperin) or played as a triplet, in both France and Germany; that the quarter note was occasionally equal to three sixteenths (e.g., Les Amusemens, 2nd Rondeau, 7th Ordre, F. Couperin); that the figure eighth-sixteenth-sixteenth, could be rendered as a triplet in a texture of even eighths intended for inequality procedure; and that the note or notes following a dotted note had a similar free and adjustable performance value, irrespective of the tempo, thus promoting the idea of the variable dot and flexible notation in general. The following chapters will shed more light on the question of the dot and the triplet.

Bach and Inequality

The older style of keyboard playing, dating from approximately 1550 to 1630, was, by definition, broken or unslurred. Bach did not play in this manner, but used what was termed by G.L. Gerber a "legato" style, i.e., the addition of slurs to note groupings. This does not mean that Bach slurred together large portions of measures, or measures themselves (as was commonly thought in the 19th century and the "uninformed" 20th century).

Example 127: French Suite No. 6, Prelude, S. 817

Bach did not always write in slurs, even though it is clear from internal evidence that he intended them. We see this in the cantatas. Bach (or a student) marked these parts himself, since they were performed by people beyond his immediate control. His family and students would have been familiar with his style and did not need these markings as would players unfamiliar with his style. As the cantatas were performed by others, he often marked the string parts himself to make his intentions clear. Here we often find slur markings placed over groups of 2, 3, or 4 notes, less often over 6, 7, or 8, and rarely over 12 notes. The fastest note values in each piece are so marked. Eighth notes are rarely marked unless they are in pairs or in groups of four on a single note. Larger values than 8ths (in a 16th note texture) are almost never marked. Therefore, when Bach is said to have played in "legato" style, this means that he slurred the groupings of the fastest notes, usually 16ths, in various ways. As we saw in the qualifications of Quantz and Couperin, when groupings are slurred, they are not played in inequality. The addition of slurs to larger groups, but not to pairs of notes, precludes inequality. This is a good indication that, except for French-modeled works, *Bach did not use inequality as a general performance style* in his own playing.

Bach, historically, could have employed inequality procedures in several ways: 8th note textured compositions written in the French organ mass style; works like Courantes, having French antecedents; compositions featuring Courante rhythms and signature (3/2, occasionally 6/4), within an 8th note texture. Most French dance music was played at a brisk tempo, thus eliminating inequality procedure. The Courante, however, was a moderate tempo dance. The 8th note-textured Sarabande would also qualify for inequality.

The *Prelude in C Sharp Minor,* WTC I, has an 8th note texture and a 6/4 signature, and sounds well with a gentle (3:2) inequality throughout. Experiment, using both SL and LS rhythms.

Example 128: Prelude in C Sharp Minor, WTC, I, S. 849

The "figure" texture of pairs of 8ths beginning in m. 4 of the *F Sharp Minor Fugue,* WTC I, is most conducive to SL inequality treatment.

Example 129: Fugue in F Sharp Minor, WTC I, S. 859

In addition, any works which match French overture texture should be played in inequality, within the "Lullian" conventions of inequality and upbeat synchronization as described by Muffat and Quantz. (The fastest general note value should be played in inequality—LS—Bach's 16ths correspond to Muffat's 8ths in Overture texture; here, the figure of the 16th rest followed by three 16ths should be "rushed" to the next beat.)

Also included would be works which are overture-like in texture, or which use a "French" model. The following are somewhat more daring in their alterations of the original, and should be considered experimental:

Example 130: Prelude in B Minor, S. 544 (original)

Example 131: Fantasia in C Minor, S. 537 (original)

Example 132: Prelude in B Minor, S. 544

Example 133: Fantasia in C Minor, S. 537

In the *B Minor Prelude* (Example 130), the rhythms are "moved up" to the beat as we surmise overture style was realized.

In the *C Minor Fantasy* (Example 131), the 8ths are played in inequality throughout; the slurred pairs are played as SL.

There are several ways to explain the existence of different metrical versions of the same work from Bach's pen: 1) he possibly had different metrical concepts of the same material at different times in his life; 2) he regarded the material transcribed for the harpsichord to be suited to an SL treatment (as in the second example); 3) he played this same material the same way on the violin but used slurs over pairs of notes in a "convention" sense, i.e., assuming that anyone playing would understand the SL inequality. I feel the last explanation is the true one.

Slur Patterns

It is my feeling that slurred pairs in Bach are often performed in a gentle-SL.

Here are two works, each with the same music, but in two differing versions, with different rhythm treatment. The example in D minor is the later version.

Example 134: Magnificat, S. 243, No. 3: Quia Respexit

Example 135: Concerto in D Major, Second Mvt, m. 23, S. 1054

Example 136: Concerto in E Major for violin, same measures as above, S. 1042

Example 137: Typical Slur Patterns

Slurring often transversed beats within the measure, very occasionally across the bar line. (This was done to insure the dominance of the downbeat.) Proper articulation or realization of slurred groups is of utmost importance in the realization of correct stylistic — metric, signature and rhythmic — performance concepts of the 18th century. These considerations take precedence over the 19th century "long line" concept. It is interesting to note that as the tempo increases so does the necessity of slurred groups in keyboard music. A detached style can only be executed at a moderate tempo.

In addition to slurrings, one confronts other articulation problems: overholding notes through a texture to indicate voice leadings, especially in slower music, e.g., allemandes. Long notes (half notes and whole notes) were usually played less than their written value.

Dotted Notes

As we have seen in the discussion of inequality, notes written evenly should, within certain limitations, be performed as if they were dotted or similarly altered. This is not because the notational symbols used in dotting were unknown or unused, but as a labor saving device in a time when all music had to be copied by hand.

The notational convention for dotted notes in the Baroque was that the note(s) following the dotted note are equal to the value of the dot. However, the relative length of the notes and the dot was considered variable. Etienne Loulié, 1696, an important French source on inequality, dotted notes and other rhythmical questions, gives us several possibilities.

The Dot

Ordinarily, a dot after a note augments its value by half. Sometimes, it augments the note by one-eighth, or one-quarter, or three-eighths, or one-half, or five-eighths, or three-quarters, or seven-eighths. That is to say that the dot of a quarter note sometimes has the value of a thirty-second note [A], or a sixteenth note [B], or three thirty-second notes [C], or an eighth note [D], or five thirty-second notes [E], or three sixteenth notes [F], or seven thirty-second notes [G].

Example 138: Loulié: Eléments de la musique, p. 67 (Albert Cohen's translation)

So a figure written as ♩. ♪ could be played in any ratio from ♩ ♪ to ♩... ♪, depending on the context. This does not mean that dotted notes had to be realized in one of these varied ways. They could also be realized quite literally, again dependant on the context.

C.P.E. Bach gives us an interesting rule. He said that in a group of eight 32nd notes the figure ♩. ♪ is played literally. Therefore, the

D Major Fugue from the *Well Tempered Clavier* I should not be over-dotted.

Example 139: Fugue in D Major, WTC I, S. 850

The figure  is almost always realized as

Passages that have against are sometimes realized together, both as or any of its variants.

Sometimes the figure will be played , especially in overture textures.

Example 140: Clavierübung II: Overture, S. 831

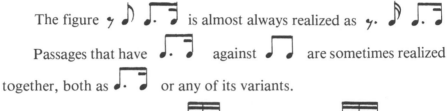

played

The reader is referred to Quantz, Chapter V, #21 for his detailed discussion of overdotting.

This variability of note values in the realization of dotted rhythms, like the variability of the ratios in equality, stems from the Baroque tradition of rhythmic flexibility.

Here is an interesting 19th century example of the overdotting problem in the *Ad Nos* Fantasy for organ of Franz Liszt:

Example 141: Liszt: Ad Nos Fantasy

Here, the second version of the figure in the pedal line is certainly played as the first (in parenthesis in the edition).

Example 142: Liszt: Ad Nos Fantasy

Overture Style

Recent evaluation of the theory of overdotting and upbeat figure synchronization as presented by Arnold Dolmetsch in 1916 (The Interpretation of the Music of the 17th and 18th century) has led to a flurry of articles, both for and against the Dolmetsch assertions.

The French Overture texture consists of two outer, slower and majestic sections, flanking a faster middle one, usually in fugal style. Sometimes the third section is very short or even non-existent. The time signature for the first section is most often C, or 2 or ₵. The tempo of the opening section, generally played too slowly, is, as given by Loulié in 1696, 56-60 to the *half* note. At this point it is important to distinguish between two differing types of textures in the first section: a.) the texture made up of quick runs and fast upbeat notes, and b.) the texture made up of constant, evenly notated fast moving notes (16ths in Bach, usually 8ths in French music). I would adopt pulse to the quarter note in this type.

It is, I believe, the first type Loulié is speaking of when giving his tempo marking. In this case the tempo remains constant throughout. The texture of notes in the fugal section changes and note values become more constant, giving the effect of an increased tempo. In two well known instances of the "a" style in Bach's music, the Overture in B Minor from the *Clavierübung II,* and in the opening movement to the fourth *Partita in D Major,* the fugal section is in triple meter. In these two cases, keeping the beat throughout produces a note-value texture one and one-half times faster than the opening, since six 16ths of the fugal section will equal four 16ths of the opening.

The second type of overture style, exemplified by Bach in the first, third and fourth orchestral suites, and by Handel in the opening of the *Water Music*, is played (according to Muffat's commentary on Lully's style) in inequality throughout, perhaps with the figure ♪♪♪ changed to ♪♩.♪ . In this second type the tempo is literally doubled from the first part to the fugal second part, because of the texture. Sometimes both textures of overture style are intermingled. In this case I would consider the proper tempo to be Loulié's suggested one.

The Loulié tempo should, perhaps, be slowed down somewhat for complex textures.

Quantz's statement about overdotting and rests, quoted on p. 118, is preceded by three important French sources: Gigault, in his *Livre de Musique Pour Orgue,* 1685, gives examples of both overdotting and upbeat synchronization, saying that if a 16th and 8th note are placed together, then they must be played together. Monteclair, in his treatise of 1736, gives clear examples of overdotting; and Hotteterre, in 1737, gives the directive that the dot of a quarter note is equal to the dot of an 8th in movements where the 8ths are unequal. Concerning the degree of dotting, St. Lambert says in 1702: "There are pieces where it seems well to make them [8ths] very uneven." (The reader is referred to John O'Donnell two articles on Overture style in Early Music Magazine, July, 1979) Using these examples in favor of the dotted style, one need simply add the usual French trill style: a breath before the termination of the trill, known as *point d'arrêt,* the stopping point most conveniently occuring at the point where the dot starts to add value to the note.

The clearest evidence of upbeat figures being played faster than written within the Bach tradition is the B Minor Overture from the *Clavierübung II.* An earlier version exists in C minor with slower upbeat figures:

Example 143: Clavierübung II: Overture, S. 831a

Clavierübung II: Overture, S. 831

The later version has upbeats sharpened, probably for clarity in publication, and a new key, possibly for reason of affect. The two versions would certainly be played in the same manner, with the 16ths in m. 13 played in inequality.

Triplets

John Banner, also known as Gianantonio Banner, wrote in his *Compendio Musico II* (Padua, 1745), "Observe in composing never to put three notes against two, this being one of the most forbidden musical situations." This categorical statement reflects the style of the period which did not allow in general and for the most part for the occurrence of two-against-three, or a three-against-four. Literal realization of these figures would be unlikely in the music of this period. Three-note figures of either duple or triple meaning were known as "figura corta": ♩♩♩ , or ♩♩♩ or ♩♩♩ ; and could, under certain circumstances, be used interchangeably.

Marpurg (1755) makes the following comment in his *Anweisung...* p. 24:

> It is frequently customary to employ simultaneously a simple and a composite measure, for example 12/8 against C as well as 6/8 against 2/4, or 9/8 against 3/4, and so forth. If in this combination of measures two notes of equal value occur against three others likewise of equal value, for example, two eighth notes against three other eighth notes, or two quarter notes against three others, the first two of the three equal notes will always be played against the first of the two.

Example 144: Partita in E Minor, S. 830: Gavotte

Duplets must often be altered into triplets, for instance, in certain dance movements; gigues are shown to be in triple context in choreographies and in triple meters (6/8 or 9/8, for example). Some of the earliest examples of gigues written in duple meter (with later versions of

the same in triple meter) in keyboard suites occur in Froberger. The
following are two examples from Bach.

Example 145: First French Suite, S. 812: Gigue

Written:

Played:

That Bach wrote duplets (intending triplet performance) before breaking into written triplets, is wonderfully demonstrated by the horn call in
Brandenburg Concerto No. 1, S. 1046, first movement, written in the score:

but performed in the original horn call:

Example 146: Sixth Partita, S. 830: Gigue

Written:

Played:

Since the individual notes of a duplet are notated in the same way as the individual notes of a triplet, we see odd things in the notational practice of Bach and his contemporaries, where sometimes duplets and triplets are written for apparently the same figure. The following example from Telemann, *Cantata No. 25* for voice and violin, illustrates this.

Example 147: Telemann: Cantata No. 25 for voice and violin

mich,   wei -

In measure 24, the voice has six quarter notes to a bar, and the violin has four. To avoid two against three, they are performed as follows: the second quarter of the ♩♩ is played together with the second note of the ♩♩♩ figure. Thus we know that the rhythmic figure ♩♩ throughout this piece is intended to be performed ♩♩𝄾 (triplet 3), including the places where there does not happen to be a two against three. This interpretation is influenced by the "Presto" as well as the slurring.

It is possible that one of the reasons for this—to us—odd notational practice of writing "duplets" and triplets for the same figure, was the result of the convention governing time signatures and tempo.

If Bach wanted a passage to be performed ♫♫ ♫♫ but did not employ 32nd notes, fearing the performer might regard the 32nd notes as the basic value, and therefore play much too slowly, he could write (triplet 3) ♫♫ ♫♫. It was assumed, then, that the performer would choose the correct tempo for the piece, but would not play two against three, as this simply did not belong to the musical vocabulary of the period. In this way Bach could be quite sure that his notation was clear and would produce the desired tempo and rhythmic pattern.

This notation occurs many times in the *Fifth Brandenburg Concerto*. The triplets in the following passage are often heard performed as three against two, but this historical evidence argues well that they should actually be performed: ♫♫ ♫♫

Example 148: Brandenburg Concerto No. 5, S. 1050

Another problem occurs in the figure ♩. 𝄾 . In slow-to-moderate tempi, the 16th will follow the last note of the triplet, as if it were the last note of a group of six 16ths. In faster tempi, the 16th will be played with the last note of the triplet, assimilated, as it were, into the rhythm.

In this example (fast tempo) from the *Toccata in G Minor* the figures in question are beamed together.

Example 149: Toccata in G Minor, S. 915

The reader is urged to read Michael Collins' article on this subject, listed in the bibliography.

Embellishments and Ornaments

The words "embellishment" and "ornament" are often used interchangeably today, but we will use them to apply to two quite separate elements. Ornaments could be indicated by standardized notational signs, such as

w or **ᴧ** , and there are many examples of tables which give exact directions for the realization of each ornamental sign. This is the often-cited table given to Wilhelm Friedeman Bach by his father:

Example 150: Table of Ornaments from Klavierbüchlein für Wilhelm Friedeman Bach

Cadence ornaments ♩. ♪♪ or ♩. ♪ , were often left out, to be filled in by the performer.

The following is the table of ornaments by d'Anglebert, which Bach rewrote for his own needs:

Example 151: Henry D'Anglebert's "Pièces de Clavecin," 1689. "Marques des Agréments et leur signification"

Embellishments or diminutions, on the other hand, were decorations originally improvised by the performer. For instance, a passage written as

Example 152: English Suite in G Minor, S. 808: Sarabande

could be performed as

Example 153: Les agréments de la même Sarabande

but another performer, or even the same performer at a different time, might perform it as

Example 154

A performer confronted with the ornamental sign would have no such freedom. The only notes he could possibly play would be

Example 155

If we look at the variations Bach wrote on the Sarabandes, we can

learn something about his feeling for embellishment. The following example from the *English Suite in A Minor* illustrates this:

Example 156: English Suite in A Minor, S. 807: Sarabande

When there are repeats of binary movements, we can embellish or add ornaments in this way, though perhaps with less elaboration.

Generally, we can say that Händel left embellishment more to the performer than Bach did. Bach tended to write out the embellishments he would prefer, and was criticized by his contemporary, Scheibe, for this.

The addition of ornaments and embellishments, where they are not written in by the composer, is dependent on knowing what the composer has written in other, similarly embellished passages, and the necessity of proper metric stress.

Ornaments punctuate; embellishments decorate.

Ornamentation is possible in all voice parts. Normally, the top part is most often ornamented, but all structurally important voices can be ornamented. This is certainly required in the playing of fugues, where the fugue subject must be ornamented in the same place in all successive introductions of the material. This does not mean that the same ornament must necessarily be used each time, or even that the ornament should be of the same length as the initial one; Bach, for example, imitated short trills in the pedals. The ornamented area of the subject must be ornamented throughout the fugue, even if minimally.

The Realization of Ornaments

Trills should be played on the beat and for the most part from the upper note. If approached from the step above, they will be played on the main tone in fast tempi, on the upper tone in slow tempi. If slurred to the previous tone, they will start on the principal note—before, on, or after the beat, depending on the context.

Example 157: English Suite in F Major, S. 809

In this passage it is difficult, because of the tempo, for the ornament to be realized as a trill on the beat starting on the upper note. If the trills are slurred, or if there is implied slurring, then they start on the main note but off the beat, before the beat in a fast-tempo context, and after the beat in a slow context. The same probably applies to mordents:

Example 158: Goldberg Variations, S. 988

Trills can be shortened to a single appoggiatura, as mentioned by C.P.E. Bach.

When approached from the lower neighbor, one may fill in the interval of a third with a passing tone.

In French music a trill on a long note is started slowly and the speed is soon increased to its fastest tempo. (A "train style," starting slowly and gradually gathering speed, is not what is meant here.)

Trill endings — there are two ways to end a trill:

1) The trill stops before its note value ends, then there is a break, called "point d'arrêt," and the ending ("Nachschlag") or anticipation is added. This method is mentioned in many French ornament tables. Bach wrote an *Overture nach Französischer Art* in the Second Part of the *Clavierübung,* in which he writes the trills with rests:

Example 159: Partita nach Französischer Art, S. 831

The other way to end a trill is with no such break before the ending. In such cases, the trill is written in one slur with its termination:

Example 160: Schmücke dich, o liebe Seele, S. 854

It is better not to count the beats in a trill, or to practice counting them, unless it is a short trill.

Mordents ⁗ are executed as follows:

The number of repetitions depends on the length of the note.

Appoggiaturas: The true appoggiatura is always on the beat. The Italian word tells us that the appoggiatura is leaning (slurred) onto the note following it. The length of the appoggiatura depends on the context. Quantz says that it should receive half the value of the main note, two-thirds if the main note is dotted. I believe the long appoggiatura belongs to the newer "galant" style and that J.S. Bach's style is short and occasionally before the beat. The appoggiatura is always slurred into the next note and is slightly louder when played on an instrument capable of dynamic variations. The appoggiatura is sometimes shown as a small hook (or double hook ⁽⁾ (circling the note), but most frequently as a small note. There are ornamental passing tones incorrectly termed appoggiaturas. These notes are played before the beat and are frequently found in French music. Context, then, determines whether a small note is an appoggiatura or a passing tone.

Sometimes in Bach's music, we find instances in which a small note, treated as an appoggiatura, would create parallels if played on the beat. In these cases, I would play the small note before the beat.

Example 161

Example 162: The Canonic Variations on Vom Himmel hoch, S. 769

The length of the appoggiatura is from one-fourth to one-half the value of the note to which it is attached, or one-third to two-thirds the value of a dotted note.

The Schleifer (two ascending steps, ꟷ) may be played on or before the beat, depending on the context. French composers frequently write the Schleifer as two small notes before the main note, suggesting by the notation that it be played before the beat.

Here's an example from Bach, written out on the beat:

Example 163: Trio Sonata in D Minor, organ, Third Mvt., S. 527

written out before the beat:

Example 164: Allein Gott in der Höh sei Ehr, S. 662

The arpeggio  indicates that a chord should be broken upwards, downwards, or both. Bach does not give directions for the roll or the chord, although Couperin does.

Diagonal strokes written between the notes of a chord indicate that the passing tone should be added. The whole chord, with passing tones, is arpeggiated:

Dots or dashes indicate that a note or chord should not receive its full value but is shorter. In textures that involve inequality procedures, the dot or dash above the note indicates equality and not necessarily a "separated" performance.

Cadenzas

The use of cadenzas originated in 17th century Neapolitan opera. The Latin word means "the falling" and is used by 17th century writers to describe "the musical or rhythmical fall of the voice." At a fermata, or other conventionally determined places, the soloist would introduce an improvisation designed to demonstrate his abilities as a virtuoso. This practice was considered indispensable in English and Italian music, though the French never admitted it. Quantz speculates that the reason for the omission may have been that cadenzas were "still not the mode when Lully left Italy; otherwise he might also have introduced this ornament among the French." (Quantz, Chapter XV, No. 2) However, it appears, from other sources, that Lully knew of the cadenza but simply objected to its use. As he was in almost dictatorial control of music in France, the practice never spread there. However, Quantz states that Germans and all others who devoted themselves to singing and playing in the Italian style used the cadenza extensively.

From the three examples to follow, we see that Bach admired this Italian practice and incorporated it into his own music. However, he did not always leave the cadenza up to the imagination of the performer but often composed it into the piece.

Example 165: D Minor Concerto, S. 1052

Example 166: Chromatic Fantasy, S. 903

Example 167: F Minor Organ Prelude and Fugue, S. 534

135

There are, of course, places in other works of Bach that appear to call for a cadenza: fermata points, half cadences with pauses, and other large breaks implying the same. From the three examples cited above, we see the typical formula that Bach used:

Example 168

We can employ this formula as a model in improvising cadenzas for use elsewhere.

Quantz warns against using a cadenza more than once in the same piece. He recommends the imitation or use of themes from the piece, is against roaming into remote keys, and decries the restrictiveness of adhering to regular meter. He adds that the abuse of cadenzas by mediocre soloists was far worse than their omission.

Mattheson, representing a slightly earlier attitude than Quantz, states that if you have a good melody, you do not really need much of a cadenza (DVK, p. 150, No. 113), and attacks the "galant" composers because "one part of the melody appears to belong in Japan, the other part in Morocco."

Here are some original cadenzas for works of Bach:

Passacaglia in C Minor, S. 582

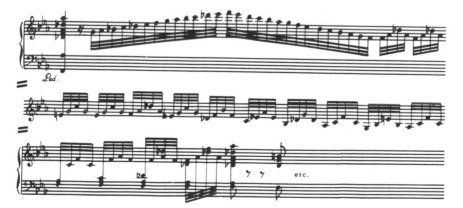

Prelude and Fugue in G Major, S. 541

Concerto in G Minor for Harpsichord and Strings, S. 1058

Dance, Dance Music
and the Baroque Keyboard Suite

with Richard Troeger

Performers today are increasingly aware of the importance of the study of dance steps and choreography and their relationship to musical styles in the Baroque period. This is of obvious value for music intended as dance accompaniment; to only a slightly lesser extent, this study can be of assistance in the rendition of stylized dance music, divorced from actual ballroom use. This chapter will outline aspects of dance steps and their relation to musical accent and tempo, and will consider the main dance movements of the Baroque dance suite.

Kirnberger tells us:

> Each of these dance types has its own rhythm, its phrases of equal length, its accents at the same places in each motif. . . .
>
> If one neglects to practice the composition of characteristic dances, one will only with difficulty or not at all achieve a good melody. Above all, it is impossible to compose or to perform a fugue well if one does not know every type of rhythm; and therefore, because this study is neglected today . . . one can no longer endure fugues, because through miserable performance which defines neither phrase nor accents, they have become a mere chaos of sounds. (Newman Powell, "Kirnberger on Dance Rhythms, Fugues and Characterization." In *Festschrift for Theodore Hoelty-Nickel,* Valparaiso University, 1967, p. 38.)

From this, it is clear that knowledge of the rhythmic nature of the Baroque dances was considered indispensable to a good performance; a useful point of departure is examination of the dance motions themselves. The arrangement of steps in relation to the meter of a given dance is helpful to a fuller comprehension of the accents and phrasing peculiar to each dance. (It is helpful, as well, to compare the music of many examples of a single dance type, and to note the points they share in common.) For the most part, French court dances were those of the Baroque-suite; we will focus attention on the most usual suite movements: the allemande, courante, sarabande and gigue, as well as some others commonly found in dance suites.

[A note on the ordering of suite movements: this varied over different periods and countries, and even from one composer to another. The first standardized ordering was that used by J.J. Froberger, Allemande-Gigue-Courante-Sarabande. Late seventeenth-century editions of Froberger's music adjusted this to Allemande-Courante-Sarabande-Gigue, which became the standard frame in Germany, with optional Prelude to begin and miscellaneous dances (often menuet and/or passepied) between the Sarabande and Gigue. In seventeenth-century France, less system is apparent; often the player must choose from a plethora of various types of movements in the same key: several allemandes, courantes, sarabandes, etc. However, the order of these groups of single dance types often conforms to the A-C-S-G pattern, rather than Froberger's A-G-C-S. This is the case in the famous Bauyn Manuscript (ca. 1660-90) and the same ordering, with preludes, opens the suites in J.H. d'Anglebert's print of harpsichord pieces (1689): suites which, after P-A-C-S-G, become each a chaos of miscellaneous movements. Eighteenth-century French suites vary from presentations resembling d'Anglebert's (Siret, 1710 and 1719) to F. Couperin's *Ordres,* varying from "standard" format (*Ordre 8*) to complete abandonment of it (*Ordre 6*).]

Baroque court dances were constructed from a common repertory of simple and compound steps, which were used in different combinations to form the various types of dance. One point which distinguishes Baroque court dance from Renaissance dancing is that, in the former, specific choreographies were composed for specific pieces. Certain features remained in common between different choreographies of a given dance, but this is distinct from the Renaissance dance's use of fixed step patterns (varying, certainly, in degrees of elaboration) which could be applied to any suitable music. It is therefore more difficult to pinpoint specific, generally applicable correlations between music and dance steps in the Baroque style; all that can be attempted here is to suggest general accentual characteristics. Even in that regard, it must be pointed out that in surviving choreographies paired with specific music, the rhythmic accents of dance and music may often be at odds; hemiolae, for example, may occur in the dance and not in the music, or *vice versa*. This independence is also true of phrase construction: measures of dance and of music will often correspond, but are not always parallel; for instance, in the passepied of Pécour's *La Bourgogne* (1700), 4 + 4 measures of music accompany a dance figure divided into 5 + 3 measures.

In most dances, whether of duple or triple meter, one step-unit was put to each measure. Exceptions were the courante and menuet (and hence the passepied; see below). John Weaver's 1706 translation of Feuillet's *Orchesographie* puts it thus:

To Tunes of Common or Triple Time, a Step is put for each Bar or Measure; and to Tunes of Quadruple Time, you must put two.

It is to be observ'd nevertheless, that in Courant Movements, two Steps are put to each Barr or Measure; the first of which takes up two parts in three of the Measure, and the second takes up the third part; and in the Minuet, one Step is put to two Barrs or Measures. (p. 47)

Thus, the courante is characterized by two stress accents per measure (usually on the first and third half notes of 3/2; see below) and the menuet and passepied are phrased in two-measure groups. Most other dances place one step-unit to the measure, or to the half-measure in quadruple or compound time.

The smallest divisions of the dance steps which make up the larger *pas simples* and *pas composés* (in turn organized into specific choreographies) are as follows. (I indicate with them Meredith Ellis Little's abbreviated notation signs ["The Dances of Jean Baptiste Lully", Ph.D. diss, Stanford, 1967, p. 99.], which allow indication of a dance's steps alongside of a line of music.)

Motion	Sign	Characteristic	Description
Plié	⌄	Upbeat; non-accentual	The knees bend gently, in a preparatory motion beginning most *pas*.
Élevé	⋀	Accentual	The knees are straightened (generally from a *plié*) in a step or rise; the dancer rises on his toes.
Glissé	∿	Non-accentual	The foot slides along the floor in a direction already initiated by another step.
Jetté	⌐	Accentual	Leap, hop or jump; the sign indicates the moment of arrival on the floor.
Marché	|	Non-accentual	Walking motion following the path of a step already initiated.
(None)	•	Non-accentual	No change of weight between feet.
(None)	⊤	Accentual	Both feet together.

The Allemande

The allemande is typically the first member of a Baroque dance suite; it may be preceded by an improvised or unmeasured prelude or, as often in the works of J.S. Bach, by a large-scale, orchestral-style movement. The allemande itself may partake of an improvisatory character, particularly in the seventeenth century; some of those by J.J. Froberger are closely related to his free toccata style. In France, and again in the works of Froberger, the allemande was often a *tombeau* as well, a slow, grave lament or elegy.

The Baroque allemande took two forms: that most frequently found in art music is of slow to moderate tempo. Apparently it did not derive from dance steps, unless from the stately, march-like steps of the Renaissance alman. The latter's uniform metric accentuation seems to have led to the purely musical development characteristic of the instrumental Baroque allemande. The other type of allemande is a dance whose principal step is the *chassé,* described by Pierre Rameau (1725) as "a hop just off the ground." (∨⌐) Rameau states that

> when you have made several [hops] in succession, as in the Allemande, you make your hops consecutively without rising on one foot.... This step [the *chassé*] is flowing, because in hopping you gain ground to perform the figure required by the dance. It has a gay effect when several are made in succession, for the dancer appears to be always off the ground, and with but a half spring. (Pierre Rameau, *The Dancing Master,* trans. Cyril Beaumont, New York: Dance Horizons, 1970, pp. 100-1.)

Like the Renaissance alman, the movement of such a dance obviates much accentual variety. This dance is light and rapid and has nothing to do with the usual, purely instrumental allemande. Rousseau's *Dictionnaire* of 1767 differentiates between the danced allemande and the instrumental variety. The former is "the air of a dance quite common in Switzerland and in Germany. This air, as well as the dance, has much gaiety and is in two beats [¢]." The instrumental allemande is defined as "a species of air or piece of music whose music is in 4/4 and is beaten gravely." Sebastien Brossard's *Dictionnaire* of 1703 (translated and expanded by James Grassineau, London: J. Wilcox, 1740) considers only the instrumental type: "the Allemande is a sort of grave and solemn music, whose measure is full and moving." Essentially, then, most instrumental allemandes are unrelated to dance. Harmonic and textural subtleties are the allemande's chief features, distinguishing it from the other members of the dance suite with their recurrent rhythmic groups and formulas. For this reason, different allemandes often exhibit considerable variation in tempo and, sometimes, rhythmic accent.

The Courante

Two types of courante are found in Baroque instrumental music. Although differentiated as corrente/coranto and courante, these terms are not always used discretely in the sources. Thus, for example, many of Bach's correnti are entitled "courante." The corrente is of Italian origin, and is a rapid dance in triple meter, usually 3/8. More frequently found is the French courante, usually in 3/2. This is a slow dance of great nobility; Pierre Rameau describes it as solemn and majestic, the favorite dance of Louis XIV. As a ballroom dance, it was out of favor after the 1660's, when the menuet supplanted it. Chambonnières wrote 88 extant examples, and the courante's subtlety, its rhythmic grace and complexity, kept it popular in instrumental music throughout the Baroque period.

Very few courante choreographies have survived, because the dance was out of fashion by the time choreographic notation was developed (the first system being published by Feuillet in 1700). The extant sources comprise descriptions (P. Rameau, 1725; Taubert's *Rechtschaffener Tansmeister,* 1717; and Compan, 1787) and choreographies (Pécour, 1700; Balon, 1712; Bocane, eighteenth-century; and two anonymous). (Wendy Hilton, "A Dance for Kings: the seventeenth-century French Courante", *Early Music* 5, 1977: 162-3) Taubert includes a choreography without music. Various step combinations appear in these accounts; the most important features are the usual use of *élevés* and/or *demi-jetté's* on the first and third half-notes of the 3/2 measure, and conclusion of the two step-units of each measure (see Weaver/Feuillet, above) with sliding motions of the foot (*glissés*). Little gives a diagram of Pécour's courante to *La Bourgogne,* which is excerpted below. Along with this, I have aligned steps described by Rameau, which include *demi-jettés.* Both of these step-sequences accent beats 1 and 3.

Example 169: Pécour: Courante to La Bourgogne

As Wendy Hilton points out, step combinations also occur in the sources which accent beats 1 and 2, or divide the measure in half. Thus, 3/2 𝅝 𝅗𝅥 , 𝅗𝅥 𝅝 , and 𝅗𝅥. 𝅗𝅥. are all stresses possible from the steps. Again, cross-rhythms between dance and music are possible, in this as in other dances. The variety of accent possible in the courante steps is perhaps attributable in part to the length of the 3/2 measure, the several divisions possible at its moderate tempo, and the varied juxtapositions possible with the two basic step units of unequal length. Musically, the courante developed these traits to make the most subtle and complex member of the dance suite.

The Sarabande

That tempo is variable for the Baroque court dances is perhaps proved by Charles Compan's remark in his *Dictionnaire* that "the sarabande, actually, is nothing but a menuet whose movement is grave, slow and serious." This brief treatment of the sarabande is partially, perhaps, late-century dismissal of a dance which was rather out of fashion, for the sarabande, like the other dances, is open to varied choreographies; Little gives four from Feuillet alone.

The principal feature of the sarabande is a prevalence of *élevés,* in which the dancer rises to a graceful balance. These occur on either the first or second beat of the triple meter, almost never on beat three; the beat thus stressed is often dotted, although dance and music can work at cross purposes in this regard. The pauses on the *élevés* are perhaps reflected in the typical rhythms 𝅗𝅥 𝅗𝅥 or 𝅗𝅥 𝅗𝅥 . Stress on both beats 1 and 2 of the same measure can be occasioned by a *jetté* on both, as in the following excerpt from a sarabande diagrammed by Little:

Example 170: Sarabande

Walking and *glissé* steps generally make up the other steps of this dance. The dancer moves primarily on the level of the beat (as opposed, for instance, to the frequent movement by quarter beats in the 3/2 meter of the courante); the impression is of an overall stately, walking movement prevailing despite the pauses of the *élevés*. The tempo is set partly by how long the dancer can balance gracefully on the *élevés* while maintaining the otherwise forward motion. Hemiolae, which appear for instance in the sarabandes of Lully, have no source in the dance motions, music and dance exhibiting counter-rhythms in such cases.

Sarabandes in instrumental literature may take the form of strongly rhythmic, dance-related textures (for instance, those of Bach's English Suite IV and French Suite VI). In other cases, the dance origin is much more remote, for instance in the Aria-sarabande theme of Bach's *Goldberg Variations*. Other such cases by Bach include the sarabandes of Partitas III and IV, and of the fifth French Suite. In both styles of sarabande, the rhythmic accent typical of the dance is likely to be of greater importance than the usual dance tempo; and even in those sarabandes most closely related to the dance itself, purely musical elaboration, embellishment or complexity of part-writing, may require a slower pace than an actually danceable tempo. Also, in aria-sarabandes, requirements of the individual melody may outweigh what impetus otherwise remains of the dance basis.

The Menuet and Passepied

I have included these two dances in my discussion of what are otherwise the nearly invariable members of the Baroque keyboard suite because of 1) the great frequency of their occurrence as dances optionally included in the suite; 2) their close relationship, indicative of an aspect of tempo to be considered later; and 3) the general prominence of the menuet in the 18th century. (Thus Rameau: "the *Menuet* is the most favored dance...." Compan's *Dictionnaire* devotes nine pages to its entry for the menuet.)

According to Rameau, the basic form of the menuet is one compound step, the *pas de menuet*. This consists of two *demi-coupés* (*plié/élevé*) followed by two *pas marchés sur la demi-pointe* (a walking step in which one rises on the toes of one foot, balancing momentarily with the legs together). These steps, described also by Compan (p. 232) take place over two measures of 3/4 time. In Rameau's words, "... the bars may be divided into three equal parts, the first for the first *demi-*

coupé, the second for the second, and the third for the two *pas marchés,* which should not require more time than a *demi-coupé."* Thus:

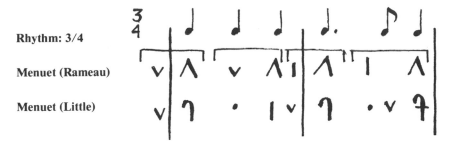

Rhythm: 3/4

Menuet (Rameau)

Menuet (Little)

Below my indication of Rameau's basic menuet step I have indicated one given by Little which involves the *pas jetté,* a little hop. Both of these patterns accent beats one and three of each measure. Simple patterns other than the two above were used and the menuet, which was very popular, was treated with a variety of embellishments and variations on its essential motions. Little remarks that the basic rhythms of the menuet

are ♩ ♩ ♩♩ , ♩. ♩♩♩ , and ♩. ♩♩ (a reshaping of the first rhythm).

Hemiolae may appear in the music, perhaps as an outgrowth of the accent on the third beat of the first measure of the triply-divided step pattern, of which the hemiola is a reflection. However, the ensuing first-beat accent in the steps does not carry the hemiola through into the motions themselves, and music and dance work essentially at cross-purposes when a hemiola appears in the former. As Rameau says, the steps divide the measures into three equal parts, but the accents do not fall completely thus.

Since the step is invariably a two-measure unit, the music of the menuet tends toward symmetrical phrasing of two or four measures (e.g., the Menuets I and II respectively of J.S. Bach's Partita No. 1 in B Flat Major); according to Little, four-measure phrases are "the main rhythmic component of 47 of Lully's 92 menuets." Irregular phrase patterns may also be found in menuet music; for example, the following combination of three-measure musical phrases with the two-measure dance pattern:

Little finds this arrangement in 27 of Lully's menuets. However, performance should keep the two-measure, ♩ ♩/♩ ♩ dance pattern in mind as its point of departure.

Tempo of the menuet would appear to be basically rather fast. Johann Kuhnau, in his *Neue Clavier-Übung, Erster Theil* of 1689, prescribes its tempo along with the rapid gigue: *"Giguen und Menueten etwas hurtig."* Quantz, in his flute tutor of 1752, puts the tempo at two quarter notes per human pulse; at his rate of pulse beat (80/minute) this comes out to ♩ = 160.

Without being particularly consistent, the tempo of the menuet seems to have slowed down in the course of the eighteenth century. Brossard calls the menuet ". . . a very gay dance, [which] comes from Poitou. We should follow the example of the Italians who use the signature 3/8 or 6/8 to mark this movement, which is always swift and very gay; the habit, however, prevails to mark it simply 3, i.e. 3/4." J.G. Walther (*Musikalisches Lexikon,* 1732) states that "the measure is in Triple Time, namely 3/4, which is usually beaten like a 3/8." The tempo would appear to have slowed down much later in the century, for thus J.J. Rousseau (*Dictionnaire* of 1767): "According to him [Abbé Brossard] this dance is very gay and its movement very swift. But, on the contrary, the character of a menuet is one of elegance and noble simplicity; the movement is moderate rather than swift and it may be said that the menuet is the least gay of all the dances used in our Ball Rooms." Charles Compan, in his *Dictionnaire* of 1787 (p. 231), quotes Rousseau's description, but goes on to say that "the measure of the menuet is of three light beats [*à trois tems légers*] marked by 3, or by 3/4, or by 3/8." The 3/8 and the *tems légers* would, then, still seem to indicate the possibility of a quick menuet tempo.

This variation in tempo possibilities will be discussed further on and is perhaps related to the menuet's own relationship to the passepied, for the latter dance uses the same step pattern as the menuet. However, it requires smaller steps taken at a faster tempo. According to Little, a variety in floor patterns, as opposed to variation in steps, is the main concern. Compan (p. 287) puts the pulse at "3/8, with one beat." He says that the passepied allows syncopation (*la syncope,* apparently in this context a hemiola) and that the menuet allows none. ("*. . . le Menuet ne l'admet point."*) Finally, "Brossard places the Passepied with the Menuet and defines it as a Menuet whose movement is faster and very gay."

Little gives an example of the passepied in her article "The Contribution of Dance Steps to Musical Analysis and Performance: *La Bourgogne* (JAMS 28, 1975, p. 115):

Rhythm: 3/8 ♪ | ♫♫ | ♩ ♪ | ♫♫♫ | ♫♫ | ♫♫ | ♩ ♪ | ♫♫♫ | ♩
Passepied: ∨ | ∧ ∨ ∧ | ∣ ∨ ∧∨ ∧ ∨ ∧ | ∣ ∨ ∧ | ∧ ∨ ∧ | ∣ ∨ ∧∨ ∧∨ ∧ | ∣
(*La Bourgogne*)

Jettés are found as well, in the place of the *élevés*. The accents fall on these; thus, with the repeated two-measure pattern of steps, emphases occur most strongly on the first beat of every other measure, making two-measure musical phrases. Again, no fully developed hemiola is found in the steps, although it is suggested in exactly the same manner that it is implied in the menuet.

The Gigue

Charles Compan (p. 165) says of the gigue that "...the measure is 6/8 and of an extremely gay nature.... This dance is no longer in use, neither in France nor Italy." The brisk motion is largely a reflection of the step accents, which emphasize the first and fourth beats of a 6/8 measure and the primary beat of a 9/8 measure. The step typically falling on these beats is the *jetté*, a leap or hop; a choreography given by Little shows accentual *pas jettés* and *élevés* on the corresponding primary beats of a compound duple meter in a 6/4 *Gigue de Roland* by Lully. Other steps in this choreography are *pliés* and *pas marchés* which fall on upbeats (beats three and four of a measure). Thus, the steps and music run closely parallel in emphasis. The *Roland* choreography, together with another step suggested by Little in her text, follow in alignment with a typical gigue rhythm from *Roland*. (Note that the *pas de bourée* is included in the *Roland* choreography.)

Rhythm: 6/4   6/4 ♪♩ | ♩. ♪♩♩. ♪♩ ♩. ♩ ♩ | ♩ ♩ ♩. ♪♩ ♩. ♩ ♩ |

Roland: (*Chassé &*   ∨ | ⌐ ∨ ⌐ ∨ ⌐ ∨ ⌐ ∨ | ∧. ∣ ∣ ∨ ⌐ ∨ ⌐ ∨
Pas de bourée)   CHASSE'   BOU REE

Contretemps: ∨ | ⌐ ∣ ∣ ∨ ⌐ ∣ ∣ ∧ | ⌐ ∣ ∣ ∨ ⌐ ∣ ∣ ∨

Any combinations of these steps are possible, individual choreographies depending on the music, or on specific music written for a preconceived choreography. The hemiolae so frequent in polyphonically complex gigues are most likely an accentual outgrowth of the *pas de bourée* and *contretemps,* with their *pas marchés* (1) on beat three; however, the step accent on beat five necessary to complete the hemiola satisfactorily is missing. The gigue hemiola (musically) apparently grew out of this implication of the steps, as is the case with menuet and passepied.

Another gigue rhythm, ♩. ♫ ♩. ♫ , is seen frequently in French and German gigues. This is a species called the *canarie.* It is highly accentual, with step accents on each dotted quarter value.

Tempo

The variation of tempo possible in Baroque court dances was touched on earlier in regard to Compan's remark that a sarabande is only a menuet taken more slowly. Another such consideration is that the passepied consists of menuet steps performed at a faster rate. That such relationships are possible is comprehensible upon consideration of the fact that the common stock of basic steps used in these dances leans heavily on various walking and flexing patterns. Balances, as in the sarabande, and numerous small leaps, as in the danced allemande and the gigue, are perhaps more apt to a close determination of tempo than the other steps. The tempo of a given dance relies, so far as can be determined from the steps themselves, on 1) the size of steps used; and 2) the particular choreography selected. A particular of the first of these concerns is mentioned by Anne Witherell (*Louis Pécour's 1700 Recueil de dances,* Ann Arbor: UMI Press, 1983, p. 80):

> At least as essential to the French technique (as posture) is the definition of the rhythm by means of the "movement," or *plié* and *élevé.* A common byproduct of dancing to very fast tempi is the elimination of the *plié.* Rameau does describe *pliés* of different depths in his treatment of the *pas composés* in *Le Maître,* although he is not very systematic about it. From this and the importance of horizontal movement in the floor pattern in the passepied . . . it seems reasonable that, in the passepied, the *pliés* might be both quicker and slightly shallower than those in the menuet. At the same time, the necessity of making a distinct *plié, place,* and *élevé* limits the speed at which the passepied might be danced.
>
> A slight difference in the depth of the *plié* seems to be a sufficient adjustment for the performance of a *pas de menuet* at a passepied tempo.

Regarding choreographies, for instance, several *jettés* in succession will require a certain range of speed, whereas an isolated *jetté* can be managed within a wider range of tempo.

As with the example of the menuet discussed above, tempo varied from one time and place to another; some contemporary authors even mentioned the wide latitude sometimes possible. Tempi should, on all occasions, be selected so as best to emphasize the beats and beat relationships of any particular movement.

A number of treatises from the later seventeenth century through the eighteenth suggest tempi for dances. These suggestions range in their nature from recommendations for specific pieces (Michel l'Affilard) or by generic type (J.J. Quantz). The tempi are given according to the human pulse (reckoned by Quantz as 80 beats per minute) or by various pendulum devices. A number of these tempi are tabulated in Table 150. Many of these will seem very fast to the modern player; it must be borne in mind that these tempi often apply to unpretentious, simply-textured compositions used for the accompaniment of actual dancing, or to similarly styled galant works, rather than to the elaborate, dance-derived music of J.S. Bach or F. Couperin.

The pendulum-based tempi of the French writers are apparently based on single motions of a pendulum: to, or fro. This is clear from a description given in 1732 by Louis-Léon Pajot, comte d'Ons-en-Bray, who remarks that a pendulum vibration lasts one second if the pendulum is of length eight feet, eight and one-half inches. Experiment based on this information readily confirms that a single, to *or* fro movement is meant by *vibration*. Erich Schwandt, in an article in the *Musical Quarterly* (Vol. 60, 1974, pp. 389-400) suggests that Michel l'Affilard, in indicating pendulum tempi, considered one vibration of the pendulum to constitute a complete to-and-fro movement. Consequently, Schwandt considers that the tempi which seem to him "incredibly fast" in their half-vibration interpretation have in actuality been interpreted by modern scholars as being twice as fast as l'Affilard intended. Schwandt is possibly correct in considering that l'Affilard misunderstood the common definition of vibration; but it is noteworthy that l'Affilard's tempi, when interpreted by the half-vibration (to *or* fro), are well in line with those of other authors who clearly used the single-motion interpretation of vibration; d'Ons-en-Bray is among these (see Table 150, which presents l'Affilard's tempi according to the half-vibration interpretation; halve the speed for Schwandt's interpretation). On the other hand, Schwandt's intrepretation puts l'Affilard well out of the mainstream of contemporary accounts of dance tempi.

As Schwandt points out, the song texts presented by l'Affilard with his dance melodies are of great assistance in understanding the accentuation of dance phrases, and should be investigated by every serious student of this music.

Table of Dance Tempi

Meter	Dance	Quantz	L'Affilard	la Chapelle	d'Ons-en-Bray	Choquel
2	Gavotte	*	♩ = 120	♩ = 152	𝅗𝅥 = 97	𝅗𝅥 = 126
	Rigaudon	𝅗𝅥 = 160	𝅗𝅥 = 120	𝅗𝅥 = 152	𝅗𝅥 = 116	𝅗𝅥 = 126
	Bourée	𝅗𝅥 = 160	𝅗𝅥 = **	♩ = 120	= 112/120	—
	Allemande	—	—	♩ = 120	♩.	—
3/2	Sarabande	—	𝅗𝅥 = 72†	—	𝅗𝅥 = 73	
	Courante	—	𝅗𝅥 = 90	—	—	—
3	Sarabande	♩ = 80	♩ = 86	♩ = 63	—	—
	Passacaille	††	♩ = 106	♩ = 63	♩ = 95	—
	Chaconne	♩ = 80	♩ = 156	♩ = 120	♩. = 53	—
	Menuet	♩ = 160	♩. = 70	♩ = 126	♩. = 70	—
	Courante	♩ = 80	—	—	♩ = 82	—
	Passepied	—	—	♩ = 152	—	—
3/8	Passepied	†††	♩. = 86	—	♩. = 100	♩. = 96
	Gigue	—	♩. = 116	—	—	—
6/4	Sarabande	—	♩ = 133	—	—	—
	Louré	♩ = 80	—	♩. = 40	♩. = 112	—
	Gigue	—	—	♩. = 120	♩. = 112	—
	Canarie	—	—	♩. = 126	—	—
6/8	Canarie	♩. = 80	♩. = 106	—	—	—
	Menuet	♩. = 75	♩. = 75	—	—	—
	Gigue	♩. = 80	♩. = 100	—	—	♩. = 104

*"a little more moderate than a Rigaudon"

**Borrel gives ♩ = 120. From the 1705 edition? No tempo given in the 1716 or 1717 editions.

†Sachs (p. 314; see Bibliography) gives ♩ = 90 (40 *tierces* as opposed to the 50 *tierces* specified in editions later than the seventh edition he used).

††"a little faster [than the Chaconne]"

†††*"slightly faster [than the Menuet]"*

Suggestions for Further Reading

Feuillet, Raoul-Auger. *Choréographie*. Paris: 1701; facs. ed. New York: Broude, 1968.

Hilton, Wendy. "A Dance for Kings: the seventeenth-century French Courante." *Early Music* 5 (1977): 160.

_____. *Dance of Court and Theatre: the French Noble Style 1690-1725*. Princeton Book Co., 1981.

Little, Helen Meredith Ellis. "Dance under Louis XIV and XV." *Early Music* 3 (1975): 331.

_____. "The Contribution of Dance Steps to Musical Analysis and Performance: La Bourgogne." *JAMS* 28 (1975): 112.

_____. *The Dances of Jean Baptiste Lully.* Stanford, Ph.D. diss., 1967.

_____. and Jenne, Natalie. *The Performance of French Dance Music.* Forthcoming.

Rameau, Pierre. *Le maître à danser.* Paris: 1725; facs. ed. New York: Broude, 1967. Trans. Cyril Beaumont. New York: Dance Horizons, 1970.

Weaver, John. *Orchesography.* London: 1706; facs, ed. Gregg Ltd., 1971.

Witherell, Anne L. *Louis Pécour's 1700 Recueil de dances.* Ann Arbor: UMI Press, 1983.

Bach's Method of Composition

On page 10, we saw how certain conclusions about performance can sometimes be drawn directly from the piece itself. One such piece is the *Organ Fantasy* and *Unfinished Fugue in C Minor.* We see there how the texture of the piece, plus a little knowledge of history, shows us the sound ideal that Bach had in mind when composing the piece, as it was modeled after pieces from de Grigny's *Livre d'Orgue.* When we say that Bach used pieces of other composers as models, it is usually the texture of the model that was used; only rarely did Bach model a composition structurally on the work of another composer. Some specific examples of this use of textures as a model are from J.K.F. Fischer, *Ariadne,* Fugues 5, 6 and 8. The themes are used quite literally, with only a slight alteration in the first one of them.

Example 171: J.K.F. Fischer: Ariadne, Fugue No. 5

WTC, Book I, G Minor, S. 861

J.K.F. Fischer: Ariadne, Fugue No. 8   Aus tiefer Not, Clavierübung III, S. 686

J.K.F. Fischer: Ariadne, Fugue No. 6   WTC, Book II, E Major, S. 878

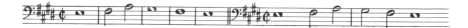

Example 172: J.K.F. Fischer: Fugue No. 3 from Prelude 2C of Der Edlern Music

Example 173: Fugue in C Minor, S. 537

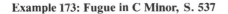

The *Erbarm' dich* for organ is modeled exactly on the texture of the *Israelites Prayer* by Kuhnau from the *Battle of David and Goliath:*

Example 174: Kuhnau: Israelites Prayer from the Battle of David and Goliath

Erbarm' dich mein, O Herre Gott, S. 721 (Authenticity questioned, the author believes it to be by J.S. Bach)

Half of the *Passacaglia* theme is by André Raison.

Example 174: André Raison: Messe Deuxième Tn. Christe

Passacaglia, S. 582

The passepied from the *B Minor Partita* from Part II of the *Clavierübung* is similar to a passepied of Couperin:

Example 175: Couperin: Passepied

Passepied from B Minor Partita, S. 831

The *Fugue* from the *Toccata and Fugue in D Minor* is borrowed from Pachelbel. The first statement in F major is quite literally from Pachelbel, as is the first half of the theme.

Example 176: Pachelbel: Fantasia in D Minor, m. 32

Fugue in D Minor, S. 565

The *C Major Organ Prelude,* S. 531, with the opening pedal solo is probably modeled after the *Prelude and Fugue in C* by Böhm.

Example 177: Böhm: Prelude and Fugue in C

Prelude in C Major, S. 531

The *G Major Prelude and Fugue* derives its material in the prelude from the *Organ Prelude in G Major* of Bruhns.

Example 178: Bruhns: Organ Prelude in G Major

G Major Prelude and Fugue, S. 550

The *G Minor Prelude* with the Allegro Fugue, S. 535, and the *Toccata in C,* S. 566, is modeled after Bruhns.

Example 179: Bruhns: Prelude and Fugue in G

Toccata in C Major, S. 566

Prelude and Fugue in G Minor, S. 535

Number Symbolism

There is much recent interest in Bach's fascinating use of numbers and number symbolism. There is room for a good deal of research in this area, as the concept of numerology, of course, invites fanciful speculation and imaginative theories. Many accidental conclusions could be arrived at, and fascinating systems have been proposed. But it is interesting that Bach used numbers in his compositions at all, and this can hardly be disputed. He signs his name occasionally in measure 14 (the sum of BACH = 2 + 1 + 3 + 8) or in measure 41 (BACH backwards and the sum of J.S. Bach), and very often these and other measures in different pieces demonstrate that he was conscious of some kind of number symbolism. Here is a good example from the *Clavierübung*, Part III:

Example 180: Vater unser im Himmelreich, S. 682, m. 41 (BACH reversed)

The texture differs from all other measures in the pedal part.

This example from *Vom Himmel hoch* shows how he signed his name:

Example 181: Vom Himmel hoch, S. 769

Bach also signs his name three times in the *Toccata in F Major;* the BACH is always transposed and never presented in its untransposed version (B flat, A, C, B).

Example 182: Toccata in F Major, S. 540

(This example was pointed out to me by Gary Schultz.)

Bach appears to use the numbers 21, 34 and 55 recurrently. (Interestingly, these are from the *Fibonnaci* series, in which each number in the series is the sum of the two previous numbers. This series is of wide interest and application in different fields of art and mathematics.) Bach sometimes uses these as the number of measures in a piece, or as the number of notes in a fugue subject.

Bach also appears to set off the numerical mid-point of large pieces. Some interesting examples: the last movement of the *C Major Trio Sonata for Organ,* S. 529:

Example 183: Trio Sonata for Organ in C Major, S. 529, last movement

In this example the scale in the right hand terminates with the downbeat of the midpoint measure. The next measure imitates the previous scale but in the left hand.

The first movement of the *E Major Sonata* for Harpsichord and Violin, S. 1016:

Example 184: E Major Sonata for Harpsichord and Violin, S. 1016

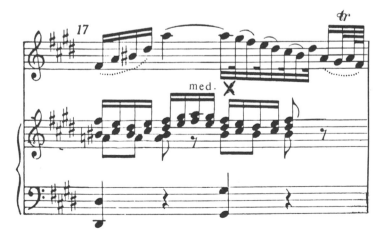

In this example we have an unusual rhythmic substitution: 4  for the time taken up by a dotted quarter note.

Example 185: G Minor Organ Fugue, S. 542

In this example, the second theme (B) begins after the midpoint's downbeat (first arrow).

The *C Minor Sonata,* fourth movement, marked by unusual slurs:

Example 186: C Minor Sonata, S. 1017

Example 187: W.F. Bach: Fugue in A Minor

In this example from W.F. Bach, we see the BACH measure, or 14 reversed (41) or the sum of W.F. Bach (sic!) set off with the dropping-out of the middle voice.

Example 188: W.F. Bach: Fugue in A Minor

In this example from the same fugue we see the midpoint (m. 92) set off with the dropping-out of the pedal voice.

From these, and many other pieces, it would appear that J.S. Bach's mature method of composing was first to determine the number of measures in the composition. Perhaps he did this in some cabalistic manner, perhaps at random, or perhaps for reasons we may never understand. Then, after setting off that number of measures on a piece of manuscript paper, if the piece were fugal in texture, he would insert the subject statements in their proper keys and voices at measure numbers that had some numerical significance to him; then the proper countersubjects would be inserted, episode material added, then any remaining missing blanks in the puzzle would simply be filled in. It appears likely that this is one way in which he was able to compose such an enormous quantity of music in such a relatively short time.

In a text of this sort it is impossible to do justice to a subject as complex as Bach's compositional processes. Alongside the mathematical computation of measures, midpoints, and number symbolism, one would also add that the harmonic direction of larger structures was probably worked out in advance. This would, of course, aid in setting up "parameters" for a composition. Heinrich Schenker has demonstrated the regularity of harmonic direction in the second half of dance movements.

Symbolism in General

with Marion Shepp

It has been suggested by historians since Bach's lifetime that Bach used symbolic language in his music. Although Bach himself never mentioned his own use of symbolism, writers as early as Mattheson alluded to "some mathematical basis of composition" in his works. In our century there has been great progress in uncovering the secrets of Bach's symbols. Schweitzer (1902) and Pirro (1907) published detailed descriptions of the "motives" in Bach's music, with their own explanations that are questioned today, for example, by Bukofzer. A key objection to their theories would be that any one motif, such as ⌐⊓ for "joy," also symbolizes several other emotions depending on the musical context. In the 1920's, the German scholar and metaphysician, Arnold Schering, continued the philosophical speculation by assigning "ultimately profound religious and spiritual values" to almost all of the known symbols. Schering likens his search for an understanding of Bach's symbols to a quest like that for the Holy Grail. Recent scholars like Smend and Geiringer are more down to earth, and have uncovered several different kinds of symbolism in Bach's writing, especially number symbolism.

Music is obviously a symbolic art, in that symbolism may be defined as a relationship between two different kinds of experience, one pointing to the other. Music symbolism is especially complicated in that it involves both the auditory symbols (melody, harmony, rhythm, tone-color, dynamics) and the visual ones, such as the notation, the form or structure of the music, selected instruments and selected performers. Musical symbolism depends upon a sensory response to music (really a primitive relationship) that is grounded in psychological and physical laws.

As suggested by Schweitzer, artistic perception involves the awakening of one's deepest feelings and ideas. Music, because it is non-specific, calls forth associations of ideas and concrete experiences that are suggested by the tones and rhythm of the music itself. All art speaks in symbols; the great artist can awaken in us the reality of existence that he has experienced, and the vital force comes from what is unspoken or unsaid. Schering says, "This means nothing more than the ability to perceive the essence of things, to sense their secret and mysterious relationships used to express even the smallest reality in musical symbols of a related nature."

Like any language, musical symbolism is understood through a

162

knowledge of its conventions. The more complex the composer's intentions, the more difficulty the untutored listener has in following them. The 19th-century music critic, Hanslick, points out that "one and the same musical passage can symbolize with equal felicitousness two emotions outside of music that appear to be of diametrically opposed natures, at least in respect of their external circumstances." So, to help make a non-specific art more specific, certain musical symbols have come into common usage. Some of these are an ascending melodic passage representing a physical ascent; a rippling passage depicting a water image; long notes for large visual objects; high and low pitches for concepts like the Resurrection and the fall of man.

Geiringer notes that "the music of Bach ... in many respects represents the glorious synthesis of artistic trends going back far into the Middle Ages." Pictorial symbolism abounded in the painting and poetry of the 17th century throughout Europe. According to the Renaissance scholar Lowinsky, secret symbolic usages had sprung up in the vocal music of the Catholic church at about the 14th century to circumvent the rigidity of the church laws governing music. The church resisted attempts to use new techniques, on the assumption that free thinking in one field of human thought could mean free or critical thinking about religion. Symbolic writing, then, could use the old symbols, but give them new meaning, known only to a few "revolutionaries" in the church musical circles.

Lowinsky continues that in the 16th century, first in the Netherlands, then throughout northern Europe, theatrical groups called Chambers of Rhetoric ("Rederijkers") began to give plays, often with large musical forces, expressing great hostility to church doctrines. In 1540, an edict was issued by the church forbidding any allusion to scripture or the sacraments in these plays. As a result, the authors and composers began to use secret techniques to depict the reformatory doctrines. Heretical books were printed under innocent titles, with fictitious authors; music was written that could be interpreted on two levels: by the common people and by the inner circle of composers and performers. Composers set words of high religious significance to new chromatic writing and modulations that made the words highly expressive. In addition, there is often evidence of humor and playfulness in matching wits with the inquisition. According to Geiringer, Magister Birnbaum, a personal friend of Bach and a teacher of rhetoric at Leipzig University, states that Bach was very familiar with rhetorical art.

It seems clear that symbolism in music was well established by Bach's time and well known to him. In this chapter we describe three kinds of symbols used by Bach in his music: I. Pictorial appearances in the score;

II. Symbolic meaning associated with musical form; and III. The use of number symbols in measures and notes, including "gematria."

I. Bach's use of pictorialism in the score is noted by Schweitzer, Geiringer and Bodky. Most of the following examples are from Bodky.

  A. Wide leaps

    1. Octave and ninth leaps describing the words "so weit" ("so far")

Example 189: Kommt es dah so weit

    2. In the *Coffee Cantata,* leaps of a ninth show the width of a beautiful skirt that the father withholds from his daughter unless she gives up coffee.

Example 190: Coffee Cantata, S. 211

    3. Octave leaps in the bass in the aria "Schlafe mein Liebster" from the *Christmas Oratorio,* S. 248, to show the rocking motion

Example 191: Christmas Oratorio, S. 248: Schlafe mein Liebster

B. Chromatic progressions
1. *St. John Passion,* S. 245, to describe the words "weeping," "malefactor," and "pushing"

Example 192: St. John Passion, S. 245

Weeping: **Malefactor:**

Pushing:

2. Falling progression at "Et sepultus est" from the *Mass in B Minor* to show the descent to the tomb

Example 193: Mass in B Minor, S. 232, Et sepultus est

3. Falling progression in the *Capriccio on the Departure of a Beloved Brother,* S. 992, to express sorrow

Example 194: Capriccio on the Departure of a Beloved Brother, S. 992

C. Walking (stepwise 8th notes)
1. *Peasant Cantata,* peasants going step by step

Example 195: Peasant Cantata, S. 212

2. *Cantata 159,* Christ's ascendance of the holy mountain

Example 196: Cantata 159

D. Cross symbols, or "chiasmus"
1. *Cantata 56,* "Ich will den Kreuzstab gerne tragen." The word "Kreuz" is sung on a note with a sharp, since in German, the sharp is called "Kreuz."
2. *St. Matthew Passion:* Judas sings, "Give me back my Lord, I pray ye." The motive by violins shows the Greek symbol for the cross, "X."

Example 197: St. Matthew Passion, S. 244

3. Bodky points out the possible symbolism of the cross in the four-note figure B flat, A, C, B (BACH) for Bach's own name. He also sees the cross symbol in several preludes and fugues from the *Well Tempered Clavier* which may seem dubious.

Example 198: WTC, Book I, C Sharp Minor Fugue, S. 849

4. The organ chorale "Da Jesus an dem Kreuze stund;" Geometric crosses in the 8th-note bass figure:

Example 199: Da Jesus an dem Kreuze stund, S. 621

5. The organ chorale "Christ lag in Todesbanden"; similar cross figures in the Easter chorale:

Example 200: Christ lag in Todesbanden, S. 625

6. From the *St. Matthew Passion,* the cross symbol, a large cross shown over the whole page:

Example 201: St. Matthew Passion, S. 244

The texture throughout forms a constant series of crosses (soli vs. tutti).

E. Flight of angels. These are melodic lines that go up and down with regularity.

   1. The organ chorale *Vom Himmel hoch,* m. 5 and 6:

Example 202: Vom Himmel hoch, S. 606

   2. Organ chorale, *Vom Himmel kam der Engel Schaar:*

Example 203: Vom Himmel kam der Engel Schaar, S. 607

F. The sound of a donkey; in the cantata, *The Contest Between Phoebus and Pan:*

Example 204: Cantata 201: Der Streit zwischen Phoebus und Pan

G. *Adam's Fall Chorale* in *Orgelbüchlein,* in which a sequence of diminished-seventh leaps shows the fall from grace to sin. Also, a writhing and wriggling theme shows the snake.

Example 205: Durch Adams Fall, Orgelbüchlein, S. 637

H. Ascending motion: In the *Gloria* of the *Magnificat,* the voices rise twice, showing God the Father and His Son. On the words "et Spiritui Sancto" the melodic line is inverted to show the descent of the Holy Ghost.

I. Descending motion, *Cantata 126:*

Example 206: Cantata 126

J. Halo effect: In the *St. Matthew Passion,* when Jesus sings, he is accompanied by a string quartet, except when he cries out, "My God, why hast Thou forsaken me?" and thus becomes a suffering human. The narrator is accompanied only by continuo.

K. Motion of waves, *Cantata 56:*

Example 207: Cantata 56: Ich will den Kreuzstab gerne tragen

II. Bach's second type of symbolism: symbolic meaning associated with musical form. We may consider, for example, A. Use of the canons;

B. Tempo changes; C. Unusual texts.

A. Use of the canon: Schering feels that by the time the canon form reached northern Germany from Italy, it had become a spiritualized form to express the greatest secrets and mystiques of religion. He says that "numerology got into a strange alliance with the canon, and God-like forces began to show themselves." Schering feels that Bach himself used the canon only as an expression of law, or of medieval, Catholic, spiritual values residual in him, even though he was so strongly Protestant.

1. In the first chorus of *Cantata 80,* "Ein' feste Burg," the fugue is framed top and bottom by a canon based on the hymn, symbolizing God's law.

2. The canon symbolizing the word "follow" ("folge") in
a. *Cantata 12,* bass aria, "I follow Jesus," strings imitate voice.
b. Aria, "Ich folge dir," from *St. John Passion;* flute and voice follow each other.

3. Duet "Et in unum Dominum" from *Mass in B Minor;* the canon at the unison demonstrates unity of the Father and the Son.

4. *Cantata 4,* chorus 5; the text refers to one death devouring another. At the end, one voice after another disappears.

5. *Musical Offering* to Frederick the Great
a. Spiral canon, modulates upward, "and may the Glory of the King rise with the rising modulation."
b. Canon in augmentation, "May the fortune of the King grow with the length of the notes."

6. The puzzle canon that Bach is holding in the painting by Haußmann. The canon is a puzzle to be solved by knowledge of "canon law."

B. Tempo change: In the organ chorale "O Mensch, bewein' dein' Sünde groß" from the *Orgelbüchlein,* Schweitzer points out that the *adagissimo* of the last bar is motivated by the words "Wohl an dem Kreuze lange" ("long He hung on the cross").

C. Unusual text: The quodlibet before the return of the Aria at the end of the *Goldberg Variations.* The words of the folksong are:

I've not been with you for so long
Come closer, closer, closer,
Cabbage and beets drove me far away.
Had my mother cooked some meat
Then I'd have stayed much longer.

In 1934, Fritz Müller "solved" the question of Bach's insertion of a song with such strange words into the magnificent variations. He says, "I" (the theme) have been away from "you" (the player) because "cabbage and beets" (the free variations) drove me away. If mother had cooked meat (if Bach had remained closer to the basic theme), I would have stayed. The return of the theme in its original form is the meat.

III. Number Symbolism in General: The third type of Bach symbolism involves the use of numbers, generally called "numerology" or "gematria." From the time of Pythagoras, the knowledge of the properties of numbers had been regarded by philosophers as a secret mystery. It was believed, even by scientists like Copernicus and Kepler, that God had arranged all things in number and measure. Early Christian mystic sects, particularly the gnostics, transmitted the use of numbers as religious symbols to the church fathers in the Middle Ages, and so to later times. St. Augustine set the number 12 (the number of apostles) as "the church." In the early 14th century, the parts of the Mass were reduced from six to five to symbolize the wounds of Christ.

Number symbolism is found in pre-Bach composers, such as Dufay, Josquin, Obrecht and Ockeghem, who used numbers as religious symbols in their vocal works. Bach probably read the writings of Andreas Werckmeister, the theory teacher of J.S. Walther, who outlined the use of numbers in music. Bach's contemporaries, Buxtehude, Mattheson and Händel, used number symbolism, and Martin Luther described the number seven as a "herrliche" ("marvelous") number. His song "Christ lag in Todesbanden" has seven verses of seven lines.

The theory of music held an important place in the writings of philosophers in the Baroque period. Gottfried Leibniz, a contemporary of J.S. Bach, emphasized the harmonic relationship of the universe. He tried to reconcile the senses and the intellect by saying that music was the "unconscious counting of the soul" and that the unconscious realization of mathematical proportions was the ultimate cause of the sensuous effect of music. Probably Bach used numbers in his own works to contribute to the order, logic and perfection that he tried to achieve in his art.

By Bach's time certain numbers had general significance:

3 Trinity
5 Wounds of Christ
6 The Creation
7 The holy number
8 Resurrection
10 The Law
11 Loyal disciples
12 The Church

Number-word symbolism, "gematria," uses both the Roman and the thesic Greek alphabet: A = 1, B = 2, C = 3, D = 4, E = 5, F = 6, G = 7, H = 8, I or J = 9, K = 10, L = 11, M = 12, N = 13, O = 14, P = 15, Q = 16, R = 17, S = 18, T = 19, U or V = 20, Z = 24.

Words often used by Bach include:

14 = BACH
29 = JSB or SDG (Soli Deo Gloria)
41 = JS BACH
43 = CREDO

Of special significance is that 14 (BACH) and 41 (JS BACH) are mirror images, and these measures often are significant. In addition, the letters BACH stand for the notes B-flat, A, C, B-natural, and these notes are called the "Bach signature."

A. Examples found by the author. It is possible to find significant number symbolism—especially by searching measures 14 and 41—and looking for the Bach signature. For example:

1. Chorale-prelude, *Nun komm, der Heiden Heiland,* S. 659. Measure 14 has 29 notes with the pitches B-flat, A, C, B-natural in reverse order on the beats, and in the pedal. Thus Bach has signed his name *three* times in one measure.

2. Chorale-prelude, *Vater unser im Himmelreich,* S. 737. Measure 14 has 14 notes.

3. *Fantasia super Komm, heiliger Geist, Herre Gott,* S. 652. Measure 14 has 29 notes. Also, measure 41 has 29 notes, if the tied note is counted.

4. Chorale-prelude, *Wenn wir in höchsten Nöten sein,* S. 641. In the first measure the melody has 14 notes, the whole measure 29. There are 158 notes in the cantus firmus, signifying Johann Sebastian Bach in gematria.

5. In the *Passacaglia in C Minor,* S. 582, in measure 29, there are 14 notes.

B. Bach's name: here are several referred examples of number symbolism using Bach's name.

1. Bach's final work, *Vor deinen Thron tret' ich hiermit ("I am appearing before Thy Throne"),* S. 668. Bach used 14 notes for the first line of the hymn and 41 for the entire melody.

2. In the opening *Kyrie* from the *B Minor Mass,* S. 232, there are 14 entrances of the fugue theme.

3. In the first fugue of the *Well Tempered Clavier,* Book I, S. 846, the theme has 14 notes, again a signature?

C. *Mass in B Minor,* S. 232

1. Patrem Omnipotentem: Randolph Currie finds a complex ar-

rangement of the number 84 in the piece, the simplest of which are the number of measures and the total letters in the text. 84 (Bach's faith) equals 41, JS BACH plus 43, CREDO. In addition to the number 84, which Bach wrote in the manuscript at the end of the piece, the numbers 14 and 41 are also woven into the music.

2. Credo. The number 43 symbolizes the Credo. In this section the word "credo" appears 43 times, and the total number of bars of the Credo and the Patrem sections is 129. This number is 43 times 3, to symbolize the three repeats of the word "credo" in the liturgy.

D. *St. Matthew Passion*, S. 244

   1. References to number of disciples (12, 11 or 10)

     a. When Jesus says that one of the disciples will betray him they say "Lord, is it I?" 24 times, or twice each.

     b. Chorus following Christ's capture. Two soloists sing, while chorus interrupts nine times. Eleven is emphasized; Judas had left the group.

     c. Peter sings, "I will watch with Jesus gladly," chorus sings refrain, "So all our sins have gone to sleep" ten times to refer to the ten disciples remaining.

   2. In 1970 Siegmund Helms published the results of his study of gematria in the *St. Matthew Passion*. He found that of the 78 pieces in this work, 55 have hidden symbols in gematria. One example of his amazing findings is:

Chorus No. 1, "Kommt, ihr Töchter, helft mir klagen" = 325. Organ II plays, after the ritornello, 325 notes. "Sehet den Bräutigam, seht ihn wie ein Lamm" = 416; Alto sings during this chorus 416 notes.

Chorale: "O Lamm Gottes unschuldig" = 245; the two flutes play 245 notes each.

   3. Jesus drinks the cup at the Last Supper. The bass accompaniment has 116 notes, referring to Psalm 116, verse 13, "I will take the cup of salvation and call upon the name of the Lord."

E. *St. John Passion,* S. 245. Pilate hands Jesus to the Jews to be judged by them. On the word "töten" ("kill"), there are five chromatically ascending notes, referring to the fifth commandment the Jews have just mentioned. The theme is repeated ten times, referring to the Ten Commandments.

F. Use of the number 6 (Creation): Geiringer proposes that Bach's continued use of the number 6 for the number of compositions in his sets: the Brandenburg Concerti, the organ Trio Sonatas, the English and French Suites, the six Partitas, the Sonatas and Suites for violin and cello, is based on 6 being the number of days for the creation of the world.

G. The number 10 (Ten Commandments): in the Fughetta on Dies sind die heiligen zehn Gebot (these are the Holy Ten Commandments), the theme appears ten times.

H. The puzzle canon that Bach wrote for his entrance to Mizler's Society, the " Correspondierende Societät der Musicalischen Wissenschaften" in Leipzig in 1747. As analyzed by Smend in the article "J.S. Bach bei seinem Namen gerufen," the puzzle contains numerical references to G.F. Handel, who was also a member of the Society, and to Bach himself. The numbers 14 and 41 are used for Bach and 8 is used for Handel's first initial, and 11 is used to indicate that Handel was the 11th member of the Society. Bach was the 14th.

In this chapter we have discussed a broad spectrum of examples of Bach's symbolism. Number symbols especially can be carried to much more complex levels that are beyond the scope of this book. However, it is very obvious that Bach, like other artists of the 17th and 18th centuries, used symbolism in his works to make them more personal. When Bach weaves his name into the fabric of the music, or when he uses numbers to relate the meaning of the words and the music, then it seems that we are part of a profound artistic and intellectual experience when we perform these works. It seems incredible that Bach would count large numbers of notes as some scholars theorize; but it does seem reasonable that he planned music in an architectural way, counting measures to determine the form of the piece, and making certain measures very meaningful. Perhaps in some instinctive way he counted the numbers of notes also. The important thing is that our understanding and performance of these masterpieces today can be enriched by the symbols of 250 years ago.

The Affect of Keys

Johann Mattheson, in *Das Neu Eröffnete Orchestre* (1713), described the characteristics of scales in regard to "affect" or passion. In this work he explains the affect of sixteen different scales. For example, he characterizes F-sharp Minor as a key more pensive than gloomy, and goes on to give other characteristics.

In general a musical work of this period featured only one affect per composition. One can easily find similar connotations of key affect in Bach's music: e.g., B minor is usually slow and pensive; D-sharp minor is slow and gloomy; D Major is clear and bright, etc. Later composers of the Classical period also assigned color significance to keys.

Bibliography

Schering, Arnold, *Bach und das Symbol,* (*Bach Jahrbuch,* 1925, p. 40-65.)

Smend, Friedrich, *Johann Sebastian Bach bei seinem Namen gerufen.* Kassel, 1950.

Geiringer, Karl, *Symbolism in the Music of Bach:* a lecture delivered in the Whittall Pavilion of the Library of Congress, May 23, 1955. Washington 1956.

Lippman, Edward Arthur, *Symbolism in Music.* (*Musical Quarterly,* October 1953, p. 554-575.)

Schering, A., *Das Symbol in der Musik,* Leipzig, Koehler and Amelang, 1941.

Lowinsky, Edward Elias, *Secret Chromatic Art in the Netherlands Motet,* New York, Columbia University Press, 1946.

Bodky, Erwin, *The Interpretation of Bach's Keyboard Works,* Harvard University Press, Cambridge, Mass., 1960.

Currie, Randolph N., *A Neglected Guide to Bach's Use of Number Symbolism, Part II,* (The Journal, *BACH,* Jan. 1974, pp. 36-44.)

The Transition to Classicism

The transition to the "galant" style and to Classicism was, as are most artistic transitions, a gradual one. We have seen that important musicians, such as Quantz and L. Mozart, though thoroughly trained in the Baroque traditions, were already in the beginnings of the transition to a new style.

There are two basic differences between the Baroque and Classical styles. The first is that in Baroque music the alternations of strong and weak measures are often irregular while in Classical music they are for the most part regular. One notices this especially in the music of W.A. Mozart. The flowering (rising) of the melody is often on the weak measure.

Example 208: W.A. Mozart: Sonata in B flat

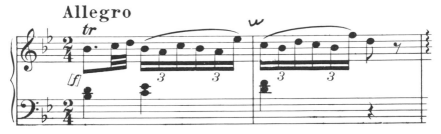

The second important difference is that in the new style the music is dominated by the treble line. There is not much imitation in the bass or inner voices and not much invertible counterpoint. Thematic contrasts eventually emerge as a stylistic characteristic, but only later (1760s) in the classical period. In Baroque music each composition features only one "affect."

The origins of Classicism are probably in Italy in the early 1700s, with the music of Sammartini, Durante, Galuppi and others. In France, treble-dominated music with little bass imitation already occurred in the galant style in the early 1700s and continued with its peculiar stylizations until the 1790s. A characteristic late French composer of this period is Duphly.

The performance of strong and weak structural subdivisions is talked about as late as 1802 in the second edition of *Klavierschule...* by Daniel Gottlob Türk. He advocates the use of dynamic

177

changes for the indication of strong and weak alternations, rather than changes in duration of notes, and is a helpful source for tempi.

There is a well known story about Beethoven and W.A. Mozart. Beethoven was asked to comment on Mozart's playing. He said that he admired Mozart's playing but felt it was "too choppy" ("zerhacht"). I find this to be an interesting statement because it is apparently a criticism of Mozart's Baroque performance style or stylistic hangovers (the holding of strong measures, structural beats, articulation of note groups, and the first note of slurrings). This style of Baroque performance was certainly learned by the young Mozart from his father. Thus when Beethoven said that he found this style of playing "too choppy," he was probably reflecting the ending point—the dissolution of Baroque performance practices. Coming from a figure as great as Beethoven, that statement was a final "Amen!"

Mozart himself used both techniques—rubato and dynamic stress—in the performance of his music. Dynamic markings, slurs or texture changes in Classicism sometimes act as contra-indications to the normal strong and weak beat and measure patterns that would be expected as the norm in Baroque tradition.

W.A. Mozart often places an *f* on a measure that would normally be weak to indicate that he did not want the typical Baroque alternations of strong and weak. Beethoven went further and actually broke down the whole concept of alternating strong and weak. Beethoven used *f* and *sfz* (an accelerated messa di voce) as means for dislodging the beat. Viewed from the perspective of the Baroque, he placed accents against the normal accent pattern of the measure.

We have mentioned Beethoven's description of Mozart's playing as choppy ("zerhacht"). Czerny relates that Beethoven played the organ this way in his youth and later developed a more fluid style on the piano. Probably Beethoven was schooled in the remnants of the Baroque tradition by his early teachers.

We read that in his later life Beethoven played solely in tempo rubato. I can hardly believe this meant that his left hand maintained strict rhythm at all times while his right hand moved freely. It surely means that he moved through and held entire beats *ad libitum* according to his concept of the music.

I doubt that Beethoven's rubatos were structurally different from the kinds of rubatos used by C.P.E. Bach, or even by J.S. Bach. It is, rather, the stylistic mode of musical expressivity that was different. The way of stretching music in time was probably very similar. The approach to the metrically important point is especially significant. In Baroque and earlier Classical style the approach is in strict time or very slightly retarded. In later Classical style and the Romantic period the approach often features a ritard, often with a crescendo.

An interesting example from W.A. Mozart of usual and then unusual groupings of strong and weak measures follows:

Example 209: Mozart: Sonata in D Major, K. 576

On the "flowering" or weak measure, one played slightly softer than in the previous measure when no dynamic change was indicated. This makes the effect in these "weaker" measures "exquisite." The "flowering" of the melody in the weak measure in Classical style occurs about 60 percent of the time.

Later in the Classical period strong and weak theory and practice in musical composition became more "hearsay" than standard practice. We see later remnants in Beethoven's "Quattro" and "Tre Battute" indications. These indicate measure groupings.

Example 210: Beethoven: Opus 131, Scherzo

Also an example exists in Liszt's *Mephisto Waltz* (Liszt's numbering):

Example 211: Liszt: Mephisto Waltz

Even Artur Schnabel's edition of Beethoven's piano sonatas reflects this old practice in his "numbering" of the measures.

String Playing

Sources: Three important mid-18th century sources for information about the performance of string music in the Baroque period are Tartini, Geminiani and Leopold Mozart.

Giuseppe Tartini (1692-1770) was a violin virtuoso and composer who established a violin school in Padua. His contemporaries evidently considered him to be the greatest performer in Italy. Diderot, the French Encyclopedist, went further and called him the greatest musician of his century. Tartini's *Treatise on Ornamentation* appears to have been widely known and circulated throughout Europe. It was an influence not only on string playing but on the performance of all music during that era.

Francesco Geminiani (1687-1762) was also a violin virtuoso, composer and writer. He left Italy in 1714 and went to England where his compositions and performance were popular and influential. *The Art of Playing on the Violin* (1731) is full of specific information about Baroque performance techniques.

Leopold Mozart (1719-1787) represents both the Baroque and early Classical styles of composition. As a thoroughly trained musician he was completely aware of the specific conventions relating to the Baroque period. As a performer he was no doubt conscientious in their application to music of the old style. His *Treatise on the Fundamental Principles of Violin Playing* reflects both styles and he at times refers specifically to the "old style." Like every other violinist in Europe, he evidently studied Tartini's *Treatise* and admired it. Following the rules of the game of 18th century plagiarism, he used large sections from it in his own book without mentioning the source.

Differences Between the Baroque Violin and the Modern Violin

As was true for keyboard instruments from the end of the 18th century to the beginning of the 20th century, there was a growing demand for larger string sounds and for a more brilliant and obvious kind of virtuosity. This caused the makers of string instruments to look for ways to increase the tension on the strings.

The body of the violin used during the Baroque period does not differ substantially from the body of the modern violin. The principal differences are in the neck and in the bow. The neck of the Baroque violin was extended in a straight line from the body. In the modern violin the neck is longer and is set at a greater angle to the body. The bridge is set correspondingly higher to allow for greater tension on the strings. Inside the body of the violin the bass bar and the sound post are proportionately larger to give added reinforcement for withstanding the greater tension and to increase the resonance. Today the strings are made of gut (nylon) wound with metal, and the E string is usually made of steel. During the Baroque period natural gut strings were used. The metal wound around the gut strengthens the string so that it will not break under the greater tension. This also produces a more penetrating sound.

The modern bow is longer than the Baroque bow. The most important difference is that the balance has been shifted and the shape of the "bow" is reversed. With the Baroque bow, the simple principles of leverage cause the part of the bow closer to the hand to contact the strings with more weight; as the player draws the bow across the strings, the weight decreases closer to the tip. One plays "lower" on the modern bow. The natural dynamic of a note or passage played on a down bow will be $f > p$; the natural dynamic of a note or passage played on an up bow will be $p < f$. However, the shift of balance in the modern bow makes it easier for the player to put almost equal pressure on the strings no matter what part of the bow he is using. The modern bow was developed for playing music composed for a sound ideal which called for longer lines and gradual changes in dynamics. The Baroque bow is better suited for music created with a sound ideal of constantly shifting variations between strong and weak notes and passages, although a modern bow can with some effort produce a similar effect.

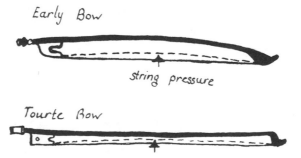

Early Bow

string pressure

Tourte Bow

More complete descriptions of the differences between Baroque and modern technique are found in Boyden, *The History of Violin Playing...*, London, 1965, and Babitz, *Six Solo Sonatas: Bach,* Early Music Laboratory, Los Angeles, 1972. The following summary briefly describes three primary areas of contrast substantially affecting the sound ideal: bowing, vibrato and attack.

We see that the physical changes in the bow itself were made during the 19th century in order to serve a different sound ideal, in order to eliminate the evident differences in dynamic between up and down bowing. The symbols ⊓ (down bow) and ∨ (up bow) apparently derive from the Latin words "nobilis" and "vilis," or perhaps as symbols for the "frog" and "tip" of the bow; they are synonyms for "strong" and "weak." Other symbols were also used: ✕ or P(oussez) for down bow; and T(irez) for up bow. The modern school of playing attempts to make the down bow and the up bow roughly equal in weight and strength, and to make the shift from one to the other as imperceptible as possible. The earlier aesthetic clearly capitalized on the difference. L. Mozart constantly uses the terms "downstroke" and "upstroke" interchangeably with the terms "strong" and "weak." "As melody is a constant varying and mixing, not only of higher and deeper, but also of longer and shorter tones which are expressed by means of notes which again are restricted by a definite time measure, so must there necessarily exist rules which instruct the violinist how to use the bow properly and in such manner that by an orderly system of bowing the long and short notes will be played easily and methodically." (Chapter IV, Par. 1, p. 73)

Tartini gives as a general rule that "the strong always occurs on the first note of the quarter, eighth or sixteenth part of the measure" (p. 11, Babitz's translation). But L. Mozart's treatise goes into more detail and takes almost every possible musical pattern which could be played on the violin, giving detailed instructions as to how to determine which notes or passages should be played with a downstroke or an upstroke. These detailed instructions extend down to 32nd or 64th notes of strong and weak subdivisions of any sort, and also suggest strong and weak measures.

He is concerned with slur groupings, dotted rhythms, and different kinds of inequalities, describing how different effects can be produced through different bowings. Even within L. Mozart's own textural designations, these concerns became quite complex. The lengthy deliberations as to which kind of slur groupings on strong or weak beats or subdivisions should be played on an up or on a down bow are evidently very important to him. We can see that the music of Bach and his contemporaries must be subject to similar considerations. It was clearly of vital importance to L. Mozart, the performer, to decide when to use a down bow to give a note or group of notes the proper strength. In Chapter IV, No. 29, L. Mozart says, "if the composer has forgotten to mark the slurs or has himself not understood how to do so," then the performer must use good taste and sound judgment. This is important. We often assume that unslurred music should be played with each note bowed separately, but this assumption goes against everything that we learn from these violin virtuosi who were writing about performance practice of their times — whose lengthy discussions of bowing all were directed toward using a down bow on notes or passages that should be strong, and an up bow on notes or passages that should be weak. Exceptions to this, such as arpeggiated passages in which each note was often played with a separate bow, are described and marked in detail by our sources. Of course they did not always agree with each other. Geminiani appears to have made less use of the metrical accent than other musicians of his time. But these very differences support the conclusion "that the true manner of performing the music is submerged beneath the bare surface of the printed notes of the scores." (David Boyden, introduction to Geminiani, *The Art of Playing on the Violin,* p. vi)

Vibrato was used quite differently in the Baroque period. This is true of both singing and string playing. In the more modern styles a fairly rich vibrato is the rule rather than the exception. We are so used to hearing it that a note sung or played with little vibrato, or with none at all, sounds very strange. Aside from the fact that a strong vibrato can be of great help to the musician who cannot trust himself to sing or play on pitch, this effect, which was used consciously and sparingly for particular musical purposes as an ornament in earlier music, came to be used constantly as the 19th century sound ideal changed. No value judgment as to which type of sound is "better" is intended or implied. A romantic violin concerto would sound as dreadful without vibrato as Bach's music sounds when played with a full vibrato throughout. It is our concern here to try to discover the sound ideal for which the composer created the music.

The usage of vibrato depended on the personality of the violinist and, in general, one would have to quote each of the famous fiddle players of the Italian Baroque to discover how it was used by each of them and under what musical conditions. But of this we can be sure: it was an effect and not a general characteristic, since variation of dynamic level, dependent on metric accent, was the norm. Performance instructions indicate to us that the dynamics were constantly changing, constantly getting louder and softer depending on the position in the measure, depending on the conditions for strong and weak. Because of this, there was no need to have a constant vibrato, since the sound was constantly being varied in other ways, either by dynamic or by rhythmic alterations.

Tartini had this to say about the vibrato or tremolo. (This is one of the passages that L. Mozart honored by almost literal repetition):

This kind of ornament is by its nature better suited to instruments than to the voice. So when it occurs in the human voice, it is due to the nature of that voice. The sound of harpsichord strings, of bells, of open strings of certain good bowed insruments leaves in its natural wake an undulation in the air which has been animated by it. This undulation is caused by the vibrations of the tiny parts composing the metal, or by the continued vibration of the string set in motion . . . In imitation of this effect, one can produce this vibration artificially on [stringed instruments] with a finger held on the string, despite its being slightly lifted. If the vibrato of the finger is slow, the undulation which is the vibrato of the sound will be slow; if it is fast, the undulation will be fast. One can accordingly increase the speed of the undulation little by little by starting slowly and rendering it faster by degrees. . . . THIS ORNAMENT IS NEVER USED IN THE HALFTONE WHICH OUGHT TO IMITATE NOT ONLY THE HUMAN VOICE BUT ALSO THE NATURE OF PERFECT IN-TONATION TO A MATHEMATICAL POINT, that is to say, that the intonation ought not to be altered at all in the half-tones . . . This ornament produces a very good effect on the final note of a musical phrase, if this note is not too long. . . .

The lines (capitalized by the author, not by Tartini) are interesting because they stress the similarity between string playing and singing. Sources from this period, no matter what kind of music they are talking about, refer constantly to a singing style, or an imitation of the voice. Early in this period Christoph Bernhard (1627-1697), a student of Heinrich Schütz, in his treatise *On the Art of Singing,* gives us an unusually clear and unmistakable opinion about the vibrato or the tremulo:

. . . the tremulo is a defect (except on the organ where all the voices can tremulate simultaneously, and where it sounds well because of the alternation). Elderly singers feature the tremulo, but not as an artifice. Rather it creeps in by itself, as they are no longer able to hold their voices steady.

From this it is clear that the vibrato is one of many ornamental effects, or "artifices," which must be subject to the will and control of the performer for specific musical purposes, and must not be a general sound characteristic of the instrument.

Geminiani was not so adamantly opposed to the use of vibrato as was Tartini. He even differentiates between a vibrato made on short notes to make them sound "more agreeable," and the vibrato as an ornament. Tartini describes specific places in the measure in various passages of music where the vibrato should be used as an ornament on a strong note, but should not be used on a weak note. Babitz points out in his footnote to this passage (p. 11, Babitz translation of Tartini, footnote 40):

> Unlike the modern violin vibrato which alters the pitch about one-half step, this vibrato is very narrow, using chiefly alterations of finger pressure, something which would be inaudible on the modern violin with its greater tensions. A vibrato as slow as [Tartini describes] requires the authentic 18th century violin with a small bass bar and neck.

Attack and Messa di voce

Another important difference in the sound produced on a Baroque violin by a performer playing in the style of that era is the absence of the biting attack. The biting attack was another innovation of the 19th century, a means of getting a louder and more brilliant sound. L. Mozart writes (Chapter 5, No. 3):

> Every tone, even the strongest attack, has a small, even if barely audible, softness at the beginning of the stroke; for it would otherwise be no tone but only an unpleasant and unintelligible noise. This same softness must be heard also at the end of each stroke. Hence one must know how to divide the bow into weakness and strength, and therefore by means of pressure and relaxation, to produce the notes beautifully and touchingly.

Bernhard, the singer, gives us a precise description of this same approach to a "soft" attack, as opposed to a biting attack. In No. 10 he says:

> On whole and half notes it is customary to employ a *piano* at the beginning, a *forte* in the middle and a *piano* once more at the end, as:

Example 212:

Care must be taken not to shift too abruptly to the *forte,* or vice versa, but rather to let the voice wax and wane gradually. Otherwise, what ought to be a charming refinement will instead sound absolutely abominable.

Geminiani describes the same effect, the device known as *messa di voce,* which was first used in singing, then in string playing, and later extended to all instruments technically capable of producing the effect. In Section B2 of *The Art of Playing on the Violin,* he says:

> One of the principal Beauties of the Violin is the swelling or increasing and softening the Sound; which is done by pressing the Bow upon the Strings with the For-finger more or less. In playing all long Notes the Sound should be begun soft, and gradually swelled till the Middle, and from thence gradually softened till the End....

Quantz, Agricola and North all corroborate these descriptions of the *messa di voce* and its stylistic importance for music of this period.

L. Mozart discussed the similarities between singing and string playing in Chapter V, Nos. 12 and 13. In these paragraphs he also gives us some useful insights into the avoidance of exaggerations of the stylistic effects necessary for the performance of the music of his time.

> We must therefore [so] lead the bow from strong to weak that at all times a good, even, singing and, so to speak, round and fat tone can be heard, which must be accomplished by a certain control of the right hand, but in particular by a certain alternate adroit stiffening and relaxing of the wrist. This can better be shown than described.

(For the singer the same control is, of course, obtained by control of the breath, which has much the same relation to the vocal cords as the bow does to the strings of a violin.) L. Mozart goes on to say:

> Everyone who understands even a little of the art of singing knows that an even tone is indispensable. ... Similarly an even quality of tone must be maintained on the violin in strength and weakness. ... They are therefore by no means to be praised who express *piano* so quietly that they can scarce be heard, and in *forte* start such a rasping with the bow that no notes can be distinguished.

The Organ, Harpsichord and Clavichord

The Organ in America

The departure from Classical ideals of organ building has produced problems for American organ builders. The symptoms are evident in several areas. The attempt of most organ builders in America has been to try to provide instruments which are suitable for the accompaniment of church services as well as for solo use. They have tried to duplicate characteristics of the English and French schools of the late 19th and early 20th centuries. The result of all this has been most peculiar. Very few instruments are complete copies of earlier Classical French or German instruments. The problem is not that these organs are not suited for music, but that they are not suited for performance of the literature which was composed for the earlier types of instruments, i.e., for a certain sound ideal which the composers had in mind and which cannot be fully realized on most American organs.

One of the main problems of the "American" organ lies in the mixtures: they are weak and incomplete. In order to obtain the right intensity of sound, one has to couple a great many divisions. This results in an obscurity of line as the divisions are almost never in tune with each other. Strong mixtures, particularly on the "great" organ or the "Hauptwerk," are required in order to achieve the necessary clarity. On a classical organ one can play the main division, which has large mixtures, without any couplings and produce a very satisfactory intensity. Mattheson stated that the "great" organ should have as many as 8, 10, 12 or even 20 ranks on each note (Mattheson, DVK, p. 463).

The organ loses an immediacy, spontaneity and control with an electric key action. This means that the fingers have no direct control over the reactions in the instrument. The energy given by the performer to the music does not go through the instrument. It is quite different with a tracker (mechanical) action, where the performer is directly connected to the controlling mechanisms of the organ.

The concert hall organ, in general, is the least satisfactory of all. This is true not only in America but all over the world. Divisions are never really in tune with each other. When this problem occurs in a live room, it is somewhat concealed, but as concert hall organs are generally in a dead acoustic, the organ almost always sounds noticeably out of tune. Also, there is usually some delay in the speech of the pedal stops in relation to the manual stops. All the resultant slight irregularities that a live room would conceal are intensely revealed in the typical concert hall.

Organs that are designed for concert halls or small churches where the reverberation time is slight should also be constructed bearing in mind that the sound will be quite different if the hall is full or empty. In contrast to large stone churches with a live acoustic, the bass line tends to disappear in "small" acoustic halls when the room is filled, making it important to have additional stops that can compensate for this fact as well as for a lack of intensity in the mid-range. Curiously enough, a full hall in a dead acoustic does not affect the high mixtures in the same way. Here is a "complete" but not huge "concert hall" organ that can play any literature for the instrument as well as a smaller type of "French" organ.

I. Minimum concert hall organ, for playing symphonic literature as well as standard solo works for the organ:

Great
Flutes 16, 3⅕, 2⅔, 1⅗
Principal 8, 4, 2
Rauschpfeife III-IV (2')
Fourniture V (1⅓)
Tierce Cimbel V (½)
Cromorne 8
Tremolo

Bombarde
Bombarde 16
Trompette 8
Clairon 4
Flute 8
Principal 4
Cornet V

Swell
Gemshorn 8
Gemshorn Celeste 8
Flutes 8, 4, 1⅓, 1
Principal 4
Plein Jeu IV (1')
Tierce Cimbel III (¼)
Cornet V
Hautbois 8
Trompette 8
Clairon 4
Tremolo

Pedal
Bourdon 32, 16, 8
Principal 8, 4
Mixture VIII
Bombarde 32, 16
Trompette 8, 4

II. The smaller French-style organ, for the performance of French Baroque organ music:

Great
Flutes 16, 8, 4, 1⅓
Fourniture IV-VI
Cymbel III
Grand jeu de tierce (1⅗, 2⅔, 3⅕, 5⅓)
Principal 8, 4, 2
Cromorne 8

Positiv
Flute 8
Principal 4
Cornet V
Trompette 8
Clairon 4
Voix-humaine 8

Pedal
Bourdon 16
Principal 8, 4
Bombarde 16

On this modestly sized organ one could play almost all of the French Baroque repertoire.

Organ builders are now trying to return to the Classical ideal, but the Classical ideal is still somewhat hidden. (It is only recently that actual building descriptions of Classical organs have become easily available.) Often the copies have a miniaturizing effect. This miniaturization occurs when a smaller sounding instrument is built for a similar space, or when the reedwork is scaled down on the French-type instrument, or in closed toe or nicked mixture work, or when only one part of an instrument is copied, e.g., omitting large pedal stops. There is an ideal speaking sound for a pipe with not much tolerance for adjustment, e.g., open toes on higher principal stops, almost no nicking on the mouths, or wide (¼-²⁄₇) mouths in larger rooms.

Most of the Classical organs were rebuilt in the 19th century to allow for full chord playing and thicker sonorities. The two great Schnitger organs at Alkmaar and Zwölle are really 20th century restorations of 19th century alterations. Schnitger's organs, for example, had narrow wind channels. His instruments had a kind of "howling" effect: when a note was played, the pitch appeared to rise slightly because of narrow wind channels.

Today we are in a better position to know how the Classical organs sounded and for the art and science of organ building to progress into a 20th century concept, once the Classical ideal has been recreated. For example, a very large organ might utilize two national styles of building, and, of course, be freed of the problem of sufficient winding with an electric blower.

On Organ Playing

Whereas the harpsichord as an instrument has had both a break in the continuity of performance and building, the organ has basically continued since its beginnings, primarily as a church instrument for accompanying hymns, and providing service preludes and postludes. Only within the last 150 years, has the instrument emerged in concert halls.

Tracing the styles of organ playing and building from the late Baroque we arrive at the following: in the German Baroque of Bach's time, there were two styles of building usually associated with J.S. Bach: that of Schnitger and that of Silbermann, both families of organ builders. The Schnitger style instruments of the late Baroque had very brilliant and high principal-scaled mixture work, with more or less mild reedwork. The wind channels of the organ were narrow, and did not easily permit full chord playing on the plenum. Improvising and performing on this kind of instrument would have to take the "wind" problem into account. Undoubtedly Bach would have played the Schnitger style organ in Hamburg, where there were many large instruments, even with 32 foot stops. Since he was concerned with the "winding" of an organ, I would surmise he was unhappy with this situation in the Schnitger style instruments, and perhaps for this reason, did not make a public statement about them.

The other kind of organ associated with Bach was the Silbermann style, most notably Gottfried Silbermann. These organs had much less lavish mixture work than the Schnitger types, but instead possessed fiery French reed work. Bach gave praise to this style of building more than once.

In general the pedal boards of the German Baroque organs were much more "under" the player than is the style today, making playing with the heel almost impossible, except in slow textures. Most playing was done with alternating toes of both feet, or simply with the toe of one foot, if the tessitura was particularly high or low. Scale passages occur very rarely in music of this period, and would have been played with alternating toes. The only legato playing in the pedal part would have been either for a cantus firmus, or for an occasional slurred (eighth) note on a rhythmically important beat. Although there exist almost no directives for pedal playing during this period, the experience of playing one of these organs or a modern "faithful" reproduction will confirm the fact that the toe was used almost exclusively in pedal playing.

The manual actions were harpsichord-like in sensitivity, perhaps more so than their French counterparts, and small articulations could easily be heard and achieved on the plenum sound. The more reed work added, the less likely the clarity of an articulation plan would emerge. On smaller organs shove couplers were often found, again reflecting harpsichord style.

In the French style of writing as well as in some works of Bach, one finds arpegianndi sections, probably the organ's way of achieving the *messa di voce* effect and again reminiscent of harpsichord style.

The general style of organ playing before Bach was one of non legato articulations. Bach changed this tendency somewhat by introducing slurrings over short groupings of the fastest note (generally), in exactly the same manner as string instrument bowing schemes of the time.

A few fingerings for the period have been preserved, and the problem is discussed in the chapter on fingering.

Registrational schemes for combinations on German instruments are discussed in Peter Williams *The European Organ,* London, 1966; and the French thoroughly discussed in Fenner Douglass *The Language of the French Organ,* Yale Press, 1969. It is particularly important to note the 16 foot manual stop was present in pleno combinations, and was often found on the Great of smaller instruments. Fugues would often have been played then with 16 foot sound in the manuals. In Mattheson (DVK, 490) we read the organo pleno included virtually all the stops (except for very soft stops) on the organ (including tierces).

The French organ differed radically from the organ in Germany in the simplicity of the pedal division, and in the music written for it: basically designed to show off various sound and color combinations. The 19th century organ in France developed by Aristide Cavaillé-Coll, led to a symphonic kind of instrument, with very powerful reeds, heavy actions, and the ability to make crescendi and imitate orchestral colors. Mixtures were either lacking or weak. The present day French organ is generally a modified 19th century French organ with mixture work added, and for the most part with electric action.

In Germany, after 1750, the organ started to acquire more gravity and power (one sees $5\frac{1}{3}$ and other low mutations on the great, as well as the cornet sound available on the great), perhaps first with the work of Z. Hildebrand, a student of Gottfried Silbermann. That eventually led to the organ exemplified in the 19th and 20th century by Walcker and Sons, the power still residing in the mixture work, but with generally lower pitched mixtures than the Schnitger types.

The Harpsichord

The harpsichord has certainly fared better than the organ. This is probably because it is less expensive to produce, and therefore less subject to political pressures of churches or to pressures of committees. When Landowska (one of the first "revivalists") started performing on the harpsichord in the early part of this century, the first instrument built for her resembled a kind of piano-harpsichord. This was not a harpsichord in Classical terms, but a hybrid sort of instrument, built with metal parts like a piano but plucked like a harpsichord. Since the 1950s a Classical revival has been taking place all over the world. By now a good many builders have made faithful and at times magnificent copies of antique instruments. When the problem of miniaturization has occurred, it has happened primarily because the resonance of the old instrument has not been duplicated. The antique instruments most often copied today in this country and Europe were built by Ruckers (17th century), Taskin (late 18th century), Blanchet (18th century) and Dulcken (18th century). Some of the secrets of sonority that have been solved recently include the shaving of the soundboard, the mass of the soundboard relative to its size, and questions of scaling.

During the time of Haydn and Beethoven, especially in England, there were experiments with harpsichords that imitated the piano with a "Venetian" swell, and included machine stops (mechanical devices for making sudden register changes), as well as knee levers for making crescendi.

It is now time to investigate present day possibilities of increased sonority, perhaps using other than traditional materials. Questions of the sub or 16 foot stop come into consideration for contemporary music. At least one Classical builder, Hass, ca. 1730, featured them on his lavish instruments. The most important technical problem to be solved is that of stability — making harpsichords more stable in regard to regulation and tuning. We must also ask if a larger sound, necessary in concert halls, can come from a harpsichord without sacrificing the quality of the sound, and if smaller Classical keyboards are suited to the size of contemporary hands.

The harpsichord has recently done in its revival what the organ has not managed to do — it has established as its building code the Classical ideal. The next step is to continue from there. (See *The Harpsichord Revival,* Howard Schott, Early Music, Vol. II, 1974, p. 85.)

On Harpsichord Playing

In order to present and interpret the music, the harpsichordist has three variables at his disposal:
1. Rhythmic alteration
2. Touch
3. Articulation

These are the points of contact between the performer and the instrument. Rhythmic alteration is of course the main concern of this book. The following comments about articulation and touch apply only to the harpsichord. (Other principles apply to the fortepiano, the modern piano, the clavichord and the organ.)

Harpsichord Articulation

This term refers to the manner and degree of separation between successive notes. Zero articulation occurs when one sound stops at the same instant that the next sound starts. This effect is possible, only completely and perfectly, in electronic music. On the harpsichord it is more usual for there to be any one of a variety of possibilities to either side of this zero articulation. On one side of "zero," notes are held in order to overlap them into successive notes. On the other side, notes are separated by tiny instants of silence. (This is the "silence d'articulation" referred to by Dom Bedos.)

If one finger is kept down so the damper does not touch the string before the next note is plucked, one sound is added to the next. Pitches are being added, slightly superimposed one onto the next. This can be done to varying degrees for different effects. One simple effect is that the mechanical noise of the plucking of the subsequent note is covered. A high degree of overlapping creates a blurred effect—a halo of sound. A lesser degree creates a cantabile legato. The harpsichordist may also choose to hold or slur notes selectively for their harmonic or rhythmic importance.

When pitches are neither overlapped nor played in a perfect legato, a note is separated from the next by an instant of silence. This can make the note following the silence appear louder though actual dynamic variation is barely possible on the harpsichord.

Because sound decays more rapidly on the harpsichord than on the modern piano, a technique of articulation which on the piano would produce a simple legato would produce on the harpsichord a dry semi-staccato sound with slight silences between the notes.

It is evident that the speed of the piece affects the type of articulation chosen by the player. At a slower speed more articulation is possible than at a fast tempo. At very fast tempi, Bach occasionally marked up to 12 notes in a single slur.

From the one extreme of a blurred halo of sound, through the middle ground of zero articulation or selective note holdings, to the other extreme of a distinct separation of successive notes, the harpsichordist has this constant range of choices for each hand in the task of reaching the music through the instrument.

We can get interesting insights into the sound ideal which must have influenced the development of harpsichord technique and composition for the harpsichord if we consider the importance of the lute in earlier music. The harpsichord is in fact a large mechanical lute. It is, like the lute, soft, resonant, and double strung. A note once plucked will continue to sound until it is purposely stopped. On a lute, if consecutive notes are played on the same course, putting down a finger on the next fret will stop the sound of the preceeding note, but if a note is played on one course and then the next note on a different course, the two sounds overlap. This produced an effect called "halo dissonance," residual sound from previous pitches. A lute player can choose to finger a passage in one of several ways in order to produce more or less of this ongoing resonance, as he feels will best serve the music.

Lute tablature is written in such a way that it tells when a sound should start, but not when it should stop. The player actually cannot stop the sound without doing something deliberate to stop the strings from vibrating. The listener perceives the starting of a sound as more important than the stopping. For instance, we might perceive eight successive notes as equal 16th notes, even though some might be written to be held as dotted eighths or quarters. We would hear them starting and the overlapping resonance. When played on the harpsichord, this resonant effect is produced by holding down the keys while new notes are being sounded.

This affect was particularly important in the development of French keyboard music as it grew out of the lute tradition. The first person to be officially called a harpsichordist in France was Jacques Jean-Pierre du Chambonières, "le première claveciniste du roi." His grandfather had been a lutenist whose music was so important that his contemporaries transcribed what they heard into keyboard notation and played it on the harpsichord. Gradually, the harpsichord displaced the lute as the world got louder. The French continued to notate their keyboard music with note holdings so that the sound would continue as it naturally does on the lute.

Another reason that discriminating articulation is so important in French style music is that there is a narrower band of permissible sounds.

In French music they all have to be "beautiful." They can be fluffy or sweet, light, short, etc., but they can never be harsh or ugly. In Scarlatti (Spanish style) and sometimes in Italian style music there is a much wider range of permissible sounds, from the sweetest to the harshest. Sometimes it is even desireable to hear the wood banging under the key, or to exploit the mechanical noise of the action of the instrument.

In French style music there is also a smaller spectrum of permissible tempi. Italian style music is both faster and slower. So the performer of French style music is even more responsible for detailed and subtle control of all the possibilities of articulation.

(Many thanks to Laurette Goldberg for her help in the previous chapter.)

The Clavichord

The clavichord, one of the oldest of keyboard instruments, was used as early as the early 1500s and as late as the early 1800s. The instrument, due to its small sound, was used mainly for practice and intimate performance. Its action is as simple as possible: a tangent (T-shaped piece of metal) that "hits" a string, thereby creating its own bridge. A quiet but intense, and silvery sound is produced with this action.

The ideal sound dynamic dimension is small. Playing too softly produces a "chuck"—a click rather than a pitch. Playing too loudly produces a raising of pitch.

The peculiar and enchanting quality of this instrument lies between its normal sound and its raised-pitch sound.

The fingers are completely in command of every nuance, and this extreme sensitivity to touch produces the tendency to play in a very expressive manner, much more so than on the harpsichord. In this respect it is similar to the early fortepiano, although it is still more "expressive" than the piano.

A device peculiar to the clavichord is *"bebung"*—an undulation of a single note produced by an alternating increase and decrease of pressure on the key.

The principles of performance with strong and weak beats are especially easy to bring out and understand on the clavichord. Perhaps the most imposing music written for this instrument are the works of C.P.E. Bach. Much of the enormous keyboard output of his father can also be played on the clavichord.

Bach and the Piano

Obviously it is feasible to play Bach on the piano. This has been done for over 100 years by professionals (some brilliant and some not so brilliant), by devoted amateurs, and by dogged or delighted students — and the results have been as wide-ranging as those that accompany most human endeavors.

Most people agree that the music of Bach can be performed on any instrument, by anybody, and that some musical impact is always felt. Brandenburg concerti have been performed by musically inexperienced children in steel-drum bands in the streets of New York. Bach's music has been performed on balalaikas, by jazz choruses and by huge Romantic orchestras; and although many have been offended, many more have been powerfully affected.

There is no reason why devotees of authenticity should insist that Bach be played only on the harpsichord, clavichord or organ. People with access to a piano certainly outnumber those with access to a harpsichord or organ. Who would suggest that these people, especially students, should limit themselves to the keyboard repertoire composed after 1800?

But there is no question that there are enormous differences between the piano and Baroque keyboard instruments, and that these differences present the student, the teacher or the performer with special problems. What is the result of having only one keyboard on the instrument instead of two?—the difference in dynamic possibilities?—the difference in carrying power? There is no absolute answer to many of these questions, but the following considerations may be of help in making necessary decisions.

First, it is important to realize that even though both instruments are struck to make the strings vibrate, the piano is not an enlarged version of the clavichord, an instrument contemporary with the harpsichord and which Bach played. The pressure of the finger on the key of a clavichord can be altered to make the tone not only louder or softer, but to make it rise slightly in pitch. The effect is that with pressure, the sound becomes louder and "more intense." What we perceive as intensity is actually a slight raising of the pitch. This has to do with the method of action in the clavichord. The tangent on the back end of the key is raised against the string when the front end is depressed. The louder the sound, the higher the pitch; and the softer the sound, the lower the pitch. To play the clavichord successfully, the performer must find a normal medium of sound which is the best area of expression in which small dynamic changes are possible without pitch variation. Extreme departures from this norm will be the exception, but the performer must always be aware of the extreme sensitivity of the keys to the fingers. With the piano, once a key has been depressed, the finger has no further influence on the sound.

The most important differences between the piano and the Baroque keyboard instruments are in the areas of dynamic range and of overtone patterns. The name of the "modern" instrument (originally "forte-piano," later "pianoforte") shows that the characteristic of dynamic modification through touch was the most important one in the minds of the musicians and the instrument builders of the 18th century. The range of experimentation in instrument-building through the 17th, 18th and 19th centuries was enormous, leading to many different kinds of instruments. When we talk about "the piano," we should make a distinction between two different instruments: the forte-piano with a wooden frame, and the modern piano with an all-metal frame, and the many transition instruments in between.

Bach played on forte-pianos built by Gottfried Silbermann at San Souci, the castle of Frederick the Great in Potsdam. Bach found the treble too weak and the action too heavy, but Silbermann experimented and improved his instruments, to the extent that later Bach approved of the changes. C.P.E. Bach and J.C. Bach both performed on such instruments, and J.C. Bach preferred it to the harpsichord. We know that Frederick the Great had a large collection of pianos, unfortunately destroyed in the Second World War. Bach wrote a "Musical Offering" for Frederick the Great after his visit and it appears likely that the two large fugues from this work were composed for this kind of early piano.

But we must remember that the sound of the early pianos, with their small, leather-covered hammers, the instruments used by Mozart, Haydn and the young Beethoven, is much closer to the harpsichord sound (because of the richness of the upper partials) than it is to the sound of the modern piano with metal frame which allows for up to thirty tons of tension on the strings. This increased tension partially accounts for the great differences between the early piano and the modern piano in the areas of volume, overtones and sound duration.

The harpsichord and the fortepiano have a more developed upper harmonic series than the piano. Close position chords like will sound thicker and heavier on the piano than on the harpsichord, where the strength of the higher overtones gives the effect of spreading the sound out over a larger range of pitches. The important overtones in the piano are closer to the fundamental pitch.

During the early part of the 19th century, firms that made instruments consulted with composers and performers in efforts to develop pianos more suitable to the growing demands for larger sounds and a different kind of virtuosity. There were many ingenious engineering feats in this effort to build an instrument capable of producing the desired dynamic contrasts without sacrificing quality of the tone, but it was not until about the middle of the 19th century that a piano with an all-metal frame was built. This device, as well as felt-covered hammers and covered bass strings, totally altered the sound of the instrument and led to the piano as we know it today.

Keeping these differences in mind, how can we best use the modern piano in the performance of Baroque music? The primary question is the one having to do with dynamic variety. The dynamic variability of the instrument makes evenness of sound texture difficult, and Baroque keyboard music was generally conceived for instruments which produced an even sound texture throughout, unless altered by register changes.

As we have seen, strong beats and measures were emphasized in the Baroque style by playing them louder (on instruments such as the violin, which allowed for dynamic variation) or by stretching them in time (on instruments such as the harpsichord, which did not). So we have three possibilities with the modern piano. (1) We can pretend the piano has no dynamic range, avoid dynamic variety except where a register change would have been made on a harpsichord, and use rhythmic alterations exclusively; (2) we can make full use of the dynamic range of the piano, and because we are indicating strong beats or structural subdivisions with dynamic variation, we can avoid the rhythmic alterations. It appears to me that neither of these decision would be satisfactory, but that in each piece, almost in each passage, the performer will make the third choice, sometimes using dynamic variation, sometimes using rhythmic alterations, and usually combining the two.

As the forte-piano was beginning to be used during Bach's time, and came into its own during the "galante" or Classical period, we can be sure that the Baroquisms of rhythmic alteration were used without the slightest question in the early Classical period. From the works of Mozart and later composers it would appear that dynamic changes gradually came to substitute for rhythmic alterations. W.A. Mozart and other Classical composers often used dynamic markings in their music to contradict the normal strong-weak progressions that might have been expected by performers trained in the Baroque tradition.

Sometimes rhythmic alterations do not sound well on the piano. Note holdings (holding notes past their written value, to show voice leading) can sound peculiar, because of the greater variety in tone. Slur groupings also are difficult to produce satisfactorily on the modern piano. It is immediately apparent, when listening to the harpsichord, whether a group of notes is slurred or detached. On the piano the distinction is not very clear unless emphasis is placed on the first note of each slur group.

To what extent should the pedal be used in playing Baroque music on the modern piano? The Classical harpsichords have a natural echo sound, a live acoustic. The strings were not dampened on the aftenlengths by felt, as in the piano, so this lively acoustic was built into the instrument. The piano, in contrast, has quite a dead acoustic, and the pedal was developed to counteract this and then amplify upper partials. So it would appear to be correct to use the pedal when playing Bach, but to use it sparingly. I prefer to use a slight amplification of the pedal in playing Bach on the piano, usually for structural reasons, to emphasize strong and weak beats or measures. Try playing the first movement of the *Italian Concerto* according to our performance suggestions, adding pedal on the first beat of the strong measures.

Some passages in the keyboard music were so clearly written for the simultaneous use of *two manuals* that it is very difficult to perform them satisfactorily on the piano, and to some extent, one must simply rewrite the notes. The following example from the *Goldberg Variations* demonstrates this:

Example 213: Goldberg Variations, S. 988: Variation No. 8

On the piano this simply does not work, because the hand crossings are not "audible." This passage must be performed:

Example 214: Goldberg Variations, S. 988

Measure 7 of the eleventh variation of the *Goldberg Variations, S. 988,* shows the problem of the "interfered with" trill:

Example 215: Goldberg Variations, S. 988: Variation No. 11

On the piano we must play a shorter version of the trill.

With regard to ornamentation there is sometimes a question as to whether, again because of the dynamic possibilities of the instrument, one should use less or different ornamentation. But ornamentation has a very special flavor and should be stylistically correct, no matter what instrument one is playing. Incorrect ornamentation has a way of sounding like a stylistic bluff, or as if an uninformed person were playing. If you are playing Bach on the piano – or on the balalaika – it should be with stylistically correct ornamentation.

In the performance of chamber music we have to decide what to do about the mixture of Baroque instruments and modern instruments. This problem occurs, for instance, with the *Fifth Brandenburg Concerto.* If all of the strings are modern instruments, being played with modern bows, there is a danger that the harpsichord will be drowned out, and some people might prefer to use a piano for this reason. But I think, given the choice, that it would still be better to use a strongly voiced harpsichord, and to use fewer strings, if necessary. The upper register of the harpsichord blends better with strings. The thinness of the keyboard-writing sounds on the piano as if notes were missing. This is because the lower overtone series in the modern piano makes the tessitura sound limited and uninteresting after a short time. The harpsichord does not give this effect, not only because it is possible to change reigsters, but because the basic sound pattern is richer in the upper harmonics. For the same reason, thick chords will sound heavier on the piano than on the harpsichord. Playing the same chord in a figured bass in "open" position on the piano will help to compensate for this and give the piano texture a similar effect of "airiness."

Because of the opportunities for dynamic variation on the piano it is possible to bring out lines in a way that the harpsichord cannot. The effect of bringing out fugal entrances on a piano can be striking, and one would definitely use this strong characteristic of the piano in the service of the contrapuntal quality of the music.

Although there is not usually only one absolutely correct solution to many of these problems, the main concern should always be to consider what is the stylistically important question in the music, and then to use as fully as possible the characteristics of whatever instrument is available in order to serve that end.

Conclusion

All music is stylized in a particular way. If we have only notes on a page, and no knowledge of the style, it is almost impossible for a performer to give the proper energy to the music. (Stravinsky is the only important composer who said that he did not want his music stylized, but that it should be played exactly as written. But performers who played his works —especially his solo works—under his direction, say that this was not true. They describe the certain kinds of "affect" that he communicated to them to interpret the notes on the page.)

There is a great deal of source literature describing Baroque style and Classical styles. Romantic music has its particular stylization too, although not much was written about it at the time, so we have far less authoritative source material on it than we do on Classical and Baroque stylization.

The Baroque style is most importantly characterized by the following:

1. The music is almost never played strictly in time.

2. The rhythmic freedoms are built on the premise of strong and weak structural units.

3. The time signatures are as limiting with regard to tempo and beat pattern as are notes on the staff limiting with regard to pitch.

4. The "affect" or proper energy is produced by a recognition and understanding of the above, plus "good taste," musical gift and proper technique.

The task of the performer is not simply to play a variety of rubatos, but to evaluate the relative areas of the music and to determine what type of rhythmic freedoms or rubatos are called for. A person with talent and musical instinct who has no historical knowledge will produce memorable playing. A person with no gift and great historical knowledge will not produce music. The ideal is, of course, to provide the talented musicians and students performing today with access to the wealth of source material which is easily available and from which performance conclusions must be drawn.

Baroque music is filled with many examples of "affect." It is evident that the music is intended to convey "affect" at all times. The question is to find the proper "affect" for each piece and to use the various devices described to bring out the primary energy and focus of the piece in the most direct way. It is, above all, a proper rubato that is necessary for the proper realization of this music that was written with various kinds of duration stresses in mind. These variations were never produced mechanically. The selecting and identifying of strong measures, and of strong places within measures, is one of the most important creative problems to be solved by a performer of this music. There are often several possible solutions. The only impossible solution is that the music, except for "danced" dance music, be played with metronomic regularity. A false tradition dies slowly, however. Perhaps a single work of Bach's might be looked at to convince the skeptical performer of the necessity of time freedom in general: the *Allemande* to the solo flute *Partita in A Minor,* S. 1013, sixty-five measures of uninterrupted 16th notes. The conclusion is unavoidable!

Bibliography

Babitz, Sol. *Early Music Laboratory,* Bulletin No. 3 (Early Keyboard Fingering). No. 2 (Differences Between 18th-century and Modern Violin Bowing),
No. 4 (Concerning the Length of Time That Every Note Must Be Held), No.
1 (A Problem of Rhythm in Baroque Music). Early Music Laboratory, Box
2552, Los Angeles, California 90028.

Bach, Carl Phillip Emanuel. *Versuch über die wahre Art das Clavier zu spielen.*
Berlin, 1753. Pt. II, Berlin, 1762. Facsimile of Pts. I and II, ed L. Hoffmann-
Erbrecht. Leipzig, 1957. 2nd ed. 1969.
Trans. and ed. W.J. Mitchell, New York and London, 1949. (Pt. I impor-
tant in general; Pt. II mainly for accompaniment)

Bacilly, Bénigne de. *Remarques curieuses sur l'art de bien chanter.* Paris, 1968.
Trans. and ed. A.B. Caswell, as *A Commentary upon The Art of Proper
Singing.* Brooklyn, New York, 1968.

Bodky, Erwin. *The Interpretation of Bach's Keyboard Works.* Cambridge, Mass.,
1960.

Boyden, David A. *The History of Violin Playing from Its Origins to 1861 and Its
Relationship to the Violin and Violin Music.* London, 1965.

Buelow, George J. *Thorough-Bass Accompaniment According to Johann
David Heinichen.* Berkeley and Los Angeles, 1966.

Collins, Michael. "A Reconsideration of French Over-Dotting," *Music and Letters* L (Jan. 1969) pp. 111-23.

————. "The Performance of Triplets in the 17th and 18th Centuries," JAMS,
XIX, Fall, 1966, pp. 281-328.

Couperin, François. *L'art de toucher le clavecin.* Paris, 1716. [Enlarged ed.
Paris, 1717.]
Facsimile of 1717 ed. New York, 1969.
Ed. and German trans. by A. Linde, with English trans. by M. Roberts.
Leipzig, 1933.

Dart, R. Thurston. *The Interpretation of Music.* London, 1954. 4th ed. [same as
the 1st ed. except for an updated bibliography and a few changes in minor
details] London, 1967.

Diruta, Girolamo. *Il Transilvano. Dialogo sopra il vero modo di sonar organi, &
istromenti da penna.* Venice, 1597. [First pub. 1593] Pt. II, Venice, 1609.

Dolmetsch, Arnold. *The Interpretaion of the Music of the XVIIth and XVIIIth
Centuries,* London, 1915.

Donington, Robert. *A Performer's Guide to Baroque Music,* Scribners, New
York, 1973.

Ellis, Helen Meredith, "The Dances of J.B. Lully," Ph.D. Diss., Stanford University, 1967, and "The Contribution of Dance Steps to Musical Analysis
and Performance: *La Bourgogne.*" JAMS 28, 1975, pp. 112-24.

Hilton, Wendy. "A Dance for Kings: the 17th-century French Courante." *Early Music,* No. 2. April 1977: 161-172.

Mackerras, Charles. "Sense about the Appoggiatura," *Opera* XIV (Oct. 1963), pp. 669-78.

Mendel, Arthur, and Hans David. *The Bach Reader,* W.W. Norton, revised 1972.

Mozart, J.G. Leopold. *Versuch einer gründlichen Violinschule.* Augsburg,1756.
Facsimile of 1st ed., ed. B. Paumgartner. Vienna, 1922.
Facsimile of 1st ed. Frankfurt am Main, 1956.
Facsimile of 3rd ed. (1787), ed. H.J. Moser. Leipzig, 1956.
Facsimile of 3rd ed., ed. H.J. Jung. Leipzig, 1968.
Trans. E. Knocker. London, 1948. 2nd ed., 1951.

Neumann, Frederick. *Ornamentation in Baroque and post-Baroque Music.* Princeton University Press. 1978.

Niedt, Friedrich Erhard. *Musicalische Handleitung ... Erster Theil.* Hamburg, 1700. 2nd pt. as *Handleitung zur Variation.* Hamburg, 1706. *Musicalischer Handleitung dritter und letzter Theil.* Hamburg, 1717.

North, Roger. *Roger North on Music: Being a Selection from His Essays Written during the Years c. 1695-1728,* ed. John Wilson. London, 1959.

Quantz, Johann Joachim. *Versuch einer Anweisung die Flöte traversiere zu spielen.* Berlin, 1752. French ed.: *Essai d'une methode pour apprendre à jouer de la flute traversière.* Berlin, 1752.
Facsimile of 3rd ed. (Breslau, 1789), ed. H.-P. Schmitz. Kassel, 1953.
Trans. and ed. E.R. Reilly, as *On Playing the Flute.* London, 1966.

Schmitz, Hans-Peter. *Die Kunst der Verzierung im 18. Jahrhundert.* Kassel, 1955. 2nd ed., 1965.

Simpson, Christopher. *The Division-Violist: or, an Introduction to the Playing upon a Ground.* London, 1659.
Facsimile of 2nd ed. (1665), ed. N. Dolmetsch. London, 1955.

Tartini, Giuseppe. *Traité des agréments de la musique* [?after 1752; before 1756]. Eng. tr. S. Babitz, "Treatise on Ornamentation," Jour. RME IV (Fall 1956) 75-102.

Thompson, E.J. *A Study on Organ Registration from 1500 to 1800.* Univ. of Hartford, 1982.

Tosi, Pier Francesco. *Opinioni de' cantori antichi, e moderni.* Bologna, 1723.
Trans. J.E. Galliard, as *Observations on the Florid Song.* London, 1742.
German trans., and additions by J.F. Agricola, as *Anleitung zur Singekunst.* Berlin, 1757.
Facsimile of Tosi, New York, 1968.
Facsimiles of Tosi and Agricola, ed. E.R. Jacobi. Celle, 1966.
Facsimile of Agricola, ed. K. Wichmann. Leipzig, 1966.
Reprint of Galliard trans., 2nd ed. (1743). London, 1926 and 1967.
Reprint of Galliard trans., 2nd ed. Preface by P.H. Lang. New York, 1968.

Index